JAN - 9 2006

A Love Like No Other

A Love Like No Other

STORIES FROM ADOPTIVE PARENTS

EDITED BY

Pamela Kruger

AND

Jill Smolowe

Riverhead Books
A MEMBER OF PENGUIN GROUP (USA) INC.
NEW YORK / 2005

RIVERHEAD BOOKS
Published by the Penguin Group
Penguin Group (USA) Inc., 375 Hudson Street, New York, New York 10014, USA • Penguin
Group (Canada), 90 Eglinton Avenue East, Suite 700, Toronto, Ontario M4P 2Y3, Canada (a divi-
sion of Pearson Penguin Canada Inc.) • Penguin Books Ltd, 80 Strand, London WC2R 0RL,
England • Penguin Ireland, 25 St Stephen's Green, Dublin 2, Ireland (a division of Penguin
Books Ltd) • Penguin Group (Australia), 250 Camberwell Road, Camberwell, Victoria 3124, Aus-
tralia (a division of Pearson Australia Group Pty Ltd) • Penguin Books India Pvt Ltd, 11 Community Centre, Panchsheel Park, New Delhi–110 017, India • Penguin Group (NZ), Cnr Airborne
and Rosedale Roads, Albany, Auckland 1310, New Zealand (a division of Pearson New Zealand
Ltd) • Penguin Books (South Africa) (Pty) Ltd, 24 Sturdee Avenue, Rosebank, Johannesburg
2196, South Africa

Penguin Books Ltd, Registered Offices:
80 Strand, London WC2R 0RL, England

Library of Congress Cataloging-in-Publication Data

A love like no other / edited by Pamela Kruger and Jill Smolowe.
    p. cm.
  ISBN 1-57322-316-6
    1. Adoptive parents—Biography. 2. Adoption. 3. Parent and child. 4. Family.
I. Smolowe, Jill II. Kruger, Pamela.
  HV874.8.L68   2005   2005042140
  362.2734—dc22
  [B]

Printed in the United States of America
10 9 8 7 6 5 4 3 2 1

Book design by Stephanie Huntwork

CONTENTS

Two ♥ Encounters with the Unexpected

Three ♥ Variations on Family

L ike many adoptive parents, the birth of our families was preceded by struggle. Before Pamela and her husband traveled to Kazakhstan in 2001 to adopt six-month-old Annie, they wrestled with whether they were capable of loving an adopted child as unconditionally as they did their biological daughter, Emily. Jill's trip to China in 1995 to adopt seven-month-old Becky followed eighteen months of coaxing and badgering a husband who, already resistant to fatherhood, was adamant that he did not want to adopt.

The birth of this book, by contrast, was instantaneous and stress-free. As we were leaving a monthly meeting of New York–area women writers and editors, Pamela asked Jill, "Would you be interested in coediting a book on parenting adopted kids?" Without hesitating, Jill answered, "What a great idea! Absolutely." Though much of the evening's discussion had centered on weighing the pros and cons of particular projects, neither of us felt a need to deliberate further. Instinctively, we both knew that this was an idea whose time had not only come but was long overdue.

If you are an adoptive parent, or are considering adoption, you probably understand what we mean. While the adoption literature is thick with answers to questions about the adoption process, it is stunningly thin on matters that touch on the actual raising of our kids. Standard parenting books, meanwhile, measure children's developmental and behavioral milestones against a yardstick that may not apply to children who were adopted from orphanages or the foster care system, or at older ages. In those rare instances where adoption is mentioned, it tends to be in passing, with the same jarring follow-these-10-easy-steps brightness as that applied to potty training or normalizing sleep routines.

But as we all know, adoption issues are complex, nuanced, and ongoing. No matter how competently we address a child's concern at a given moment, it refuses to wind down tidily and disappear along with cribs, crayons, or curfews. Instead, these are issues that take root early on, then burrow deeper as our children grow older. Over time, they tend to evolve, not resolve; mature, not melt away.

Such questions first began to gnaw at Pamela when her daughter Annie turned two. The fears she and her husband David had entertained about their capacity to love an adopted child had vanished within hours of first holding Annie. But now, as they prepared to enroll Annie in Jewish preschool, with plans for her to follow seven-year-old Emily into a Jewish Sunday school, Pamela began to worry. How could she honor Annie's ethnic heritage—an intriguing, rich mix of Russian, German, and Kazakh—without making Annie feel "different" within the context of the family? Should the whole family sign on to Russian lessons? Take trips to Kazakhstan? Would such activities alienate Annie, or Emily, or both?

For Jill, the most frequent questions sprang from her growing awareness that she would never be able to gauge, let alone grasp, the significance of an unidentified birth mother's claim on Becky's imagination and heart. The first time it hit her, Becky was barely eighteen months old, long after Jill's reluctant spouse, Joe, had become a smitten, involved father. Jill was holding a friend's infant on her lap when Becky suddenly charged across the room and plowed her hands into the child, shouting, "My mommy!" In a confused moment, Jill found herself doing the calculus familiar to so many adoptive parents. Was Becky simply exhibiting the behavior of an only child unaccustomed to sharing? Was she giving voice to a rudimentary awareness of her adopted status, and signaling that she felt a need to assert or defend her claim on Jill? Was the appropriate response to provide a quick lesson in the merits of sharing and the demerits of hitting? Or might it be better to set the infant down and wrap Becky in a hug that reassured, "Yes, you are mine." Since then, such moments—and questions—have only multiplied.

If such dilemmas resonate with you, then this may sound familiar, too. Although neither of us feels inclined to seek out families that "look like ours," we both find that when we encounter other adoptive parents, we tend to become engaged in intimate, candid conversations that have a language, sensibility, and awareness all their own. Often, these dialogues help to clarify issues that are nagging at us or hovering at the back of our minds. Moreover, though neither of us regards adoption as the defining characteristic of her mother-daughter relationship—indeed, we both bristle when people refer, without cause, to our children as "adopted"—we find such discussions with other adoptive parents fascinating, edifying, and, frankly, a relief.

Why? Perhaps because through such dialogue, we affirm that we are not alone in training a special ear and eye on the words, habits, and behaviors of our adopted children. We discover that we are not overthinking or underthinking, being hypersensitive or overly zealous when we probe for subtext beneath our children's embraces and exclamations, tears and taunts. We realize that we are not crazy in thinking we possess a peculiar radar that searches for meaning where people with biological children—even those of us with our own biological children—look for none.

If you are already a parent to one of this country's more than 1.6 million adopted children under eighteen years of age (the total number of those who are older is impossible to estimate), or hope to be among the estimated 120,000 Americans who will adopt in the year ahead, you know how this special radar has a way of kicking in at the seemingly most innocent moments and raising unsettling questions that tend to linger. Take, for instance, when you bring your newly adopted son to a family gathering and notice that your usually effusive relatives seem to be steering clear of your child. Is this simply the reserve some people feel around a new member of the family? Is it an indication that your relatives will always regard your son as the "adopted" one? More disturbing, could they be picking up on your own slowness to bond? Are you perhaps still harboring preadoption reservations? Has the adoption itself given rise to fresh doubts?

Now fast-forward a few years. As you plan a family trip to this same son's country of origin, he balks. "I don't want to go. I'm an American." Does this merely reflect his fear of flying or discomfort with unfamiliar places? Is it a refusal to acknowledge his roots? Or is it the first hint of a deep-seated fear that you plan to drop him off, then return home without him? Is he nursing dark fantasies that—like his birth parents somewhere out there in the universe—you might "abandon" him? Should you plunge ahead with your travel plans anyway? Or should you postpone the trip?

What about the day your once-cheerful little girl becomes a brooding and angry preteen? "You're not my *real* mother!" she yells with a look to kill. Is she simply (okay, maybe not so simply) going through a predictable adolescent identity crisis? Is her struggle compounded by adoption issues that she is unwilling to acknowledge to you, and perhaps even to herself? What if she asks uncomfortable questions about the actual adoption? If you acknowledge there were rumors of corruption in her country of origin's adoption pipeline, will she conclude she was "stolen" from her birth parents?

And what about that birth mother, whom, in moments of distress, your daughter has imagined as the perfect parent? Do you upset her soothing fantasy by sharing that the woman was a homeless street kid? What if your child was abandoned, and the details supplied by a lawyer, orphanage, or adoption agency were speculative at best? Or perhaps you *do* know the identity and location of the birth mother. Is this the moment to make contact? To build upon an extant, but distant, relationship? If you reach out, what obligations—moral, emotional, financial—might you incur? Most important, should *you* be the one to introduce this woman into your child's life? Or is that a decision for your daughter to make when she is older?

Such moments can leave a parent yearning for input, insight, or inspiration, preferably from somebody attuned to the often unaddressed issues surrounding adoptive family life. Ask anyone else and you risk either an uninformed dose of you're-reading-too-much-into-this, or the sort of worried frown that blows your concern way out of proportion. Mostly what you want is to bounce your observations and reflections off someone who is able to discern when your adoption-related musings are little more than a sideshow to the drama of daily life—and when they *are* the drama. You crave the ear of someone who understands that while adoption is not who your child is, it is an integral piece of who he or she will become. Or perhaps you're thinking of adopting and want to know what may lie in store.

Either way, you've come to the right place. The twenty gifted writers in this anthology understand. Their concerns traverse the wide spectrum special to the roughly 2.5 percent of American families that have come together, in whole or in part, through adoption. As a group, these writers' families represent the diverse nature of the adoptive nuclear unit as it looks today in America. Scattered among ten states, the families are headed by different-sex couples and same-sex couples, single mothers and single fathers, divorced parents and parents who were themselves adopted. The children, who range from toddlers to teenagers, were adopted at a variety of ages, and come from overseas and over state lines, from orphanages, the foster care system, and the homes of blood relatives. The households represented here enlarge the meaning of the term "blended family." Some have a biracial or multiracial complexion; some involve both biological and adopted kids; some mix children born abroad with those made in the U.S.A.

Each of these original essays offers a vivid snapshot of a different aspect of the adoptive parenting experience. They are, by turns, painful and joyous, humorous and sober, provocative and poignant. While the subject matter roams broadly, all these writers share a desire to explore and probe their uncertainties, ambivalences, and passions honestly. They do not seek to offer advice. They do not intend to offer resolution. Each of them appreciates that adoption issues are far too complicated for sentimental or pat answers.

As you read, you may at times find yourself nodding in recognition or agreement. At other moments, you may find yourself arguing back at the writer, seeking to articulate a different truth born of your own experience. We say, Wonderful! Let the dialogue begin. Primarily, we hope you will find what we discovered as we edited these pieces:

through the sharing comes reassurance, reflection, and reaffirmation. All of this, we believe, strengthens our ability to parent our kids with greater intelligence, insight, and love. Of this much we are certain: when it comes to the all-important task of raising our children, the adoptive parent-to-parent grapevine has been silent too long.

P.K.

J.S.

ONE

Reflections on Birth Parents

She Is Among Us

CHRISTINA FRANK

It started in Hanoi, where we went to adopt our daughter Lucy in the fall of 2001. We spent nine days there, and during our many walks around that hot, teeming, chaotic city, I was seized frequently with a feeling that I might be in the presence of Lucy's birth mother. Was that her—the attenuated woman balancing stacks of sugarcane and chickens over her shoulder? Could this be her, the woman harassing us into buying a conical hat? What about the gracious saleslady at the store where we bought silk scarves and *ao dais* (the traditional outfit for women)?

Equal parts elation and terror overcame me each time I toyed with the possibility that I had located the person who'd given birth to the tiny beauty strapped to my chest in a Baby Björn.

This continued throughout our stay in Hanoi, me randomly scrutinizing young Vietnamese women. I tried to be discreet as I hunted for specific resemblances to Lucy, searched for a look of recognition on some woman's part—and wondered what on earth would happen if I actually hit pay dirt.

When my husband and I began the adoption process, one of the first things we were asked to do was to write a hypothetical letter to our prospective child's birth mother. It was just the kind of sappy, forced exercise that made us roll our eyes and swap private, tasteless jokes about what we might say. But we muddled through, forcing ourselves to be sincere, lest we be booted out the door of the adoption agency for lack of a suitably serious attitude.

We'd already ruled out domestic adoption, primarily because we did not want to confront an "open" arrangement, where the two sets of parents are known to each other from the get-go. Along with the lack of privacy seemed to go a scary lack of boundaries. It felt somehow cleaner and less fraught with problems to find a child from a foreign country, where there would probably be little to no information about the birth family. Of course, we knew that foreign adoption came with its own thorny set of issues: the child's loss of cultural identity, the fact that she wouldn't look like us, and the difficulties that would attend the lack of information about her background.

My birth mother obsession, however, came as a complete surprise.

At that point, my husband and I were thinking mostly about our family and ourselves. Would the baby assigned to us be healthy, alert, cute? Would we be able to love her in the same way we love our biological daughter, Olivia, who was then four? Would the sister relationship between Olivia and this child be problematic because of their different origins? I could have guessed that I'd develop some curiosity and concern about the baby's birth mother, but back then she had yet to forge her own identity in my mind. She was simply one among millions of anonymous birth mothers who produce the world's abandoned babies.

To some extent, my husband still regards Lucy's birth mother this way. He claims to be mildly curious about her. But he does not share my need to fully indulge every random thought about her.

When we left Hanoi for Ho Chi Minh City to get Lucy a visa before returning to the United States, my heart sank as I realized that my one chance to locate this woman had passed. I tried to convince myself that maybe she'd turn up in the southern city, but the scant bit of information we had made it pretty clear that Lucy had been born in or near Hanoi.

When we left Vietnam altogether, my obsessive search came to an abrupt halt. I knew that while there, I had been as physically close to this woman as I would ever be.

We've been home now for over three years. Time passes in a blur of family life—inserting juice boxes into lunch boxes, dropping off and picking up, pasting Band-Aids over microscopic injuries, reading *Mr. Brown Can Moo, Can You?* six times in a row. Months can go by when not a single thought of Lucy's birth mother crosses my mind. Lucy is as undeniably and exclusively ours, as vital a player in our tight-knit family unit as is Olivia. Lucy looks nothing like us, but she is one of us. It's easy to forget that she has a history, complete with a kinship network, that none of us shares.

Then, almost out of nowhere, a powerful feeling of needing to know more about this mystery woman will strike. It can be triggered by looking at photos from our trip (is that her, lurking in the background?) or spotting an Asian woman who resembles Lucy, or seeing an article about Vietnam in the newspaper. What is she doing *right this minute*? Suddenly, I must know, can't stand not knowing, am absolutely convinced that this day must not end without knowing.

Lucy, being only four, is of course too young to ponder her beginnings or to suspect that they differ from those of her sister. Perhaps this brief honeymoon period is what allows me the luxury to fully indulge my own thoughts and feelings. Once Lucy grasps the fact that her mommy and her birth mother are not one and the same, I may have to surrender ownership of this unresolvable mystery to her. Maybe this is my way of rehearsing for Lucy's inevitable questions.

I am, of course, versed in the positive language that adoptive parents are encouraged to employ when handling such questions. The suggested phrases sound so soothing: the greatest act of love, a courageous thing to do, a better life for you, made an adoption plan. But when you strip away that armor, the unsweetened version remains: Yes, lots of poor people do keep their babies, but Lucy's birth mother wasn't one of them. Lucy's birth mother gave her away.

Certainly, I would never volunteer this version, but I imagine a teenage Lucy arriving at these conclusions herself and then pressing me to admit that yes, on some level, she was unwanted.

The little we do know about Lucy's birth mother is contained in a brief, matter-of-fact note that she tucked into Lucy's diaper before depositing her inside a health clinic in Hanoi and walking away. It is handwritten, states the baby's name and date of birth, and refers to a "family situation" that makes raising her impossible. She requests that the baby be placed in a specific orphanage. And that's it.

Though the information is scant, one detail plagues me: Lucy was about two months old when the note was written. This suggests that her birth mother had tried to make a go of raising her. This little fact unleashes a torrent of questions. Was Lucy her first child? Was her confrontation with the shocking responsibility of caring for a newborn what changed her mind? Or does she have other children, and did this one push her family to the breaking point? Had she planned to part from Lucy right after she was born, then found the prospect of a separation impossible? Did her family threaten to disown her because the baby was illegitimate?

Then there is the absolute worst possibility: Was this woman given money to surrender Lucy?

In the past few years, "baby trafficking" scandals have shut down the international adoption pipeline in Cambodia. Vietnam also has had cases called into question. While in Vietnam, my husband and I saw firsthand how bribery can figure into even the most mundane transactions: to speed the processing of Lucy's passport, one of our facilitators slipped some cash to an official.

So the grim possibility of a baby-for-cash transaction isn't as comfortingly far-fetched as I'd like it to be. The thought of a young woman needing money that desperately or being unable to resist the promises of a sleazy wheeler-dealer is excruciating. It may be a bit Hollywoodish of me, but I envision a poor, beautiful young woman standing on the side of a dusty road, sobbing as she is forced to sell her baby, who is then taken from her arms and later dropped at the health clinic.

I truly believe this scenario is unlikely, but where would I even begin if I had to justify it to Lucy?

Hoping to extract more meaning from the note, my husband and I sought out a Vietnamese scholar after we returned home. His translation differed little from what we'd learned in Vietnam. He did say, however, that the grammar and syntax indicated that the note had been written by someone with limited education. That isn't surprising. The main reason women relinquish children in Vietnam—and anywhere else in the world—is extreme poverty. (Another common reason is the stigma of unwed motherhood.)

I wish this woman had written something explicit about her love for her baby. I genuinely believe she loved Lucy, just by the fact that she left a note at all and requested an orphanage with a good reputation. That note is a whole lot more than many adopted children end up with. But it would be nice to have actual words to help ease Lucy's doubts.

As for me, the note does nothing to satisfy my curiosity. In addition to the gnawing mystery of that two-month interval, I long to know about the obvious things: What does she look like? How does she live? Why exactly did she relinquish her baby? Does she think about Lucy now? Does she have regrets? I'd also like to know about that rarely mentioned yet essential character, the birth father. Maybe it's from him that Lucy inherited her bewitching dark eyes, her willfulness, her spirit and independence. Are he and the birth mother still together, possibly with other children? Or was it a brief, insignificant fling that led to the creation of my very significant little girl?

Do the two of them have any idea how remarkable this little girl is whom they created? Or is such a consideration the privilege of middle-class American parents who have the time, energy, and resources to notice and nurture such specialness?

If someone gave me the opportunity to meet Lucy's birth mom tomorrow, I'm not sure I would take it. Perhaps I would be too afraid of what the truth might look like. There is a comfort, after all, in creating one's own fantasy birth mother—young, beautiful, vulnerable, sweet, bright, loving. I imagine Lucy will romanticize her, too. Who wouldn't, given the choice?

For all the frustrations this woman's anonymity poses, the not knowing offers one decided advantage: she can be whoever you want her to be. My husband's parents came with us to Vietnam, and while there we all enjoyed entertaining the notion that Lucy is a descendant of royalty, or at least the illegitimate daughter of a high-level official. We didn't seriously believe that was the case, of course. But the fantasies served their purpose. They helped to account for Lucy's obvious specialness, and to divert our thoughts from the likely and heart-wrenching scenario of a desperate soul driven to a desperate act.

Even if I privately nurse my own doubts about this woman's circumstances and motives, I feel fiercely defensive when people casually voice their disapproval of her. She and I, after all, share a powerful bond: Lucy.

The first time it happened was while I was getting vaccinated for the trip to Vietnam. As the platinum-haired nurse, Eleanor—a kind, soft-spoken woman I'd known for several years—administered the shots, we chatted about my upcoming trip and the adoption. I proudly displayed the few photos we had of Lucy, expecting Eleanor to gasp at my baby's beauty and wax rhapsodic about our good luck. Instead, she sighed and shook her head. "I just *can't* imagine *how* any woman could just leave her baby like that," she said. "When I think of my grandson and how precious he is to us . . ."

It was clear that Nurse Eleanor assumed I shared her feeling. In fact, I was so dumbstruck by her response that I was practically shaking as I left the doctor's office, furious at myself for keeping quiet.

That was the first time I felt a connection, an allegiance— a responsibility, really—to Lucy's birth mother. Since she couldn't speak up for herself, it was incumbent on me to do the talking for her.

"Of course *you* have no idea how someone could do this," I wish I'd said. "*You* don't live in scathing poverty where you can barely feed yourself, let alone a baby. And *you* aren't going to be potentially disowned by your entire family if your baby is born out of wedlock. What *you* know is a comfy American world where couples go into debt to have biological children if the anticipated miracle doesn't happen naturally. Or if the woman feels the need, she can get an abortion. How dare you speak that way about a woman in whose shoes you haven't walked?"

The next time someone went down the "How could she?" road, I did manage to imply that only an ignorant fool would question the reasons behind *my* daughter's birth mother's decision. By then, Lucy was not the only new member of my family. I had come to think of her birth mother and all her biological relatives as family, too.

You might think that as a biological mother myself, I would be shocked that women are capable of abandoning babies grown in their own bodies. I'm not. Though it took eleven months to conceive Olivia, and though she was unfathomably precious to me from the second she was born, I remember those first few months of mothering as truly nightmarish, a profound jolt to the formerly childless system my husband and I had known. It went beyond the wakings, feedings, and inconsolable squalling; the roller coaster of emotions; the mastitis that shot my temperature up to 104 for three days straight. Over all that loomed the terrifying awareness of the enormous responsibility that had befallen my husband and me. Only now did we truly grasp how many sacrifices we—yes we, middle-class Americans with jobs and money and grandparents dying to help out—would have to endure for the sake of this one little child.

There were many nights during that period when, delirious with sleep deprivation, I would plan my temporary escape. Just for one blessed night, I ached to check into a nice hotel and sleep undisturbed and untouched for eight consecutive hours. Sometimes I imagined camping out in a sleeping bag on the cold stone floor near the elevators in our apartment building—anywhere that was immune to the endless needs of an infant.

Now add to this mix what many of these birth mothers face. Perhaps they must share tight quarters with countless relatives. Perhaps there is no mate, loving or otherwise, to help shoulder the burden. Most definitely, whatever the household arrangement, the exhausted new mother must contend with crushing poverty. In that light, it's not so hard to comprehend why young women in impoverished countries decide they have no other choice but to hand over their babies to people who can offer these children a better life. Abortion—the way out for millions of Western women—is simply not an option for many of these women. Low availability, high expenses, or religious strictures stand in the way.

So maybe I have my answer. Still, I'm not able to accept my own ill-informed conclusions. And there's also an aspect to my needing to know that reminds me of a two-year-old who must have the toy another child is holding simply because he can't have it. Often, I feel desperate to learn more about Lucy's birth mother just because such knowledge is unavailable to me, out of my control. A photo and a few more pieces of information might go a long way toward appeasing me.

Lucy will always have two mothers, and I am inextricably linked to the other one whether or not we ever meet. I needed her to create Lucy; she needed me to raise her.

I feel most connected to this woman on Lucy's birthday, the one day out of 365 when I'm certain she's thinking about Lucy, maybe even wondering about me as I wonder about her. Just as we were as physically close as we would ever be during my visit to Vietnam, on Lucy's birthday I sense a spiritual, real-time, across-the-oceans closeness. For those twenty-four hours, I breathe a sigh of relief, feeling that for a brief time, I have found her.

To Search or Not to Search

PAMELA KRUGER

He almost whispered it to me. "We're going to search for our daughter's birth parents," he said. Three couples, all of us who had adopted from the same orphanage in Kazakhstan eighteen months earlier, had met up in New York City with our children. The ostensible purpose was to greet an employee of our adoption agency, who was visiting New York for the first time. But it was also a chance for our children to start developing friendships with others whose lives also had begun in Ust-Kamenogorsk, a remote city in northeastern Kazakhstan.

Except for a few brief e-mail exchanges, we were all strangers. Yet somehow this father had guessed, after only a half hour of conversation, that I was one of those adoptive parents who had an intense curiosity—an obsession, my husband would later call it—about the birth parents of my daughter Annie, now four. "We found someone who does birth parent searches," he said under his breath, as the children darted around us on the playground.

At the time, I thought he didn't want the kids to overhear, but later I wondered if he might have been more worried about the reaction of the adults nearby. For as I soon would learn, while it's accepted for grown adoptees to try to find their birth families, only rarely do adoptive parents embark on a search on behalf of their children, and the few who do are often viewed with suspicion, if not open disdain, by many adoptive parents and even some adult adoptees.

And certainly he should have been concerned about the adoption agency workers' reaction. In Kazakhstan, as well as some other countries in the former Soviet Union, adoptions remain tightly closed. Kazakh law requires "people who have knowledge of the adoption" to maintain its secrecy, and it specifically mandates that they shield the identities of the adoptive parents. It doesn't, however, mention protecting the privacy of the birth parents. They are widely viewed with such contempt in Kazakhstan that many find it inconceivable that an adoptive parent would want to find *them*. I once asked an orphanage worker if any Kazakh adoptive parents had made contact with birth parents. She gave me a puzzled look, then made me repeat the question a few times until she finally realized that, yes, she had understood me. "Of course not!" was her reply.

So it was in hushed conversation that I learned for the first time about a mysterious figure who had made a little business for himself tracking down birth parents in the former Soviet Union. A Russian-English translator from Ukraine, he could be contacted only through an American intermediary and was known just by his first name, R. Adoptive parents would send him copies of their adoption documents, a letter to the birth parents, and photos of their child. From that, R. often would be able to locate and interview the birth parents, sometimes taking photos of them as well. Up until this point, R. had done searches only in Ukraine and Russia. He was about to make his first trip to Kazakhstan. If I wanted to be part of it, I'd have to act fast. He was leaving in a month.

During the car ride home, I shared bits of the story—sotto voce—with my husband, David. I wasn't worried about Annie, then two, listening in so much as Emily, our seven-year-old biological daughter. When we brought Annie home from Kazakhstan in December 2001, Emily had peppered us with questions. Why had the birth mother given Annie up? If she was so poor, why couldn't we just send her some money? There had been a certain simplicity in telling Emily that we knew nothing about the birth mom, that Annie had been given up at birth. It had put an end to the discomfiting questions. I wasn't eager to reopen that subject with Emily—at least not before I was sure how David and I planned to proceed.

I had always fantasized about returning to Kazakhstan with Annie when she was older and, with the help of a translator, solving the mystery of her beginnings. While some parents choose international adoption over domestic adoption precisely because the adoptions are closed and there is no possibility of birth parent involvement, my reasons were more pragmatic: I'd heard it would be easier—and quicker—to adopt an infant overseas. Also, it would enable me to avoid being in the dreadful position—an ethical land mine, as far as I was concerned—of having to sway the decision of an emotionally vulnerable, pregnant woman.

Yet I always felt strongly that all children have a need—and a right—to know their genetic history. While in Kazakhstan, I'd grilled everyone I could about Annie's birth family. The orphanage director and workers either knew nothing or didn't feel I should learn more than what was in the official records: Annie's birth parents' names, the fact that they had lived together, and that Annie was born in a maternity hospital in Leninogorsk, a decaying industrial city several hours away from Ust-Kamenogorsk.

After we returned from Kazakhstan, David and I both spent many hours on the Internet, researching the birth parents' names and Annie's birthplace. We learned that her birth mother's surname was German. During World War II, the Soviets had exiled many ethnic Germans who lived in Russia to Kazakhstan to toil in slave labor camps. Some of these Germans were said to be Jews. This was an intriguing surprise. Perhaps Annie, like me, had Russian and German Jewish blood? We also discovered that the fact that Annie's birth father had signed a relinquishment letter was quite unusual—birth fathers' consent is not required by law and, in fact, is rarely given. Just as in the U.S. foster care system, the birth fathers are typically nowhere to be found.

From these tidbits, I spun a romantic tale of a woman, born in poverty due to generations of Soviet oppression, who—with her loving, loyal husband—made the wrenching decision to give up their baby for adoption. On some days, I even convinced myself that these paltry bits were enough.

"At least we know some facts," I'd say. "And we have the birth parents' names so that Annie could try to track down her birth parents if she ever wants to." Then I'd rattle off the statistic I'd heard at an adoption seminar, that only 10 percent of adult adoptees actually search for their birth parents. All the while, though, I couldn't imagine that Annie wouldn't want to search, and nursed the secret hope that we—she and I—would find her birth parents someday.

Now that I knew the possibility existed, however, my mind was clouded with fears and doubts. How do we know this isn't an elaborate scam? What if this guy just concocts phony stories and photos for desperate adoptive parents, and Annie grows up believing complete lies? And what about the birth parents' rights to privacy? Was it really fair to send someone to their home, asking prying, personal questions, especially given the stigma that adoption has in their culture?

As soon as our children were in bed, the story spilled out of me. David's reaction was swift and certain: He didn't want to search. It's a Pandora's box, he argued. What if we find out something awful? Do you really think Annie would be better off knowing she was a product of rape, or God knows what else? What if we contact the birth parents and find out that they want Annie back?

I didn't put up much of an argument. The truth was, I felt as frightened as my husband did about opening this door. But now that I knew there was a real chance of finding Annie's birth parents, I also knew that it wasn't in my DNA to just forget about it. David knew that, too.

The next morning, I set out to learn all I could about R. I spoke to his American contact and some references, and read postings about him in an online adoption discussion group. Within days, I had become convinced that R. was for real. There was the fact that R. sometimes returned from his search with details—obtained from the birth mother—that the adoptive parents knew but had never shared with him. Some parents also told me that the birth parents or relatives whom R. photographed bore a close resemblance to their child. Finally, R. didn't pad his findings; if he could only find an address where a birth mother once lived, that's all you got.

I also felt reassured by the way R. conducted his interviews. From what adoptive parents told me, he seemed to be respectful of the birth families. He was careful to talk to the birth parents only when they were alone. He also had a knack for knowing how to ask sensitive questions without insulting or offending. I was amazed how many of the birth parents agreed to pose for photographs and even gave R. family photos to send to the adoptive parents and their children.

But the stories R. recounted were often deeply distressing, and alarming, leaving many adoptive parents in despair. R. didn't sugarcoat the truth. So a disproportionate number of the adoptive parents learned that the birth mothers were mentally ill or alcoholics, as well as desperately poor. Brutal abuse—physical, sexual, and emotional—was a frequent backdrop. Many of the birth fathers had spent much of their lives in and out of jail, and didn't give a hoot about some baby who was being raised in America. A few adoptive parents received frantic pleas from the birth parents for money for operations or legal matters, leaving adoptive parents in a moral quandary. Shouldn't you help the woman who gave birth to your child? Then again, how do you prevent this from becoming a slippery slope? When you adopt, how much responsibility do you have to take care of your child's birth family?

Suddenly, I found myself contemplating all kinds of scenarios, none of which I had ever imagined before, all of which I felt completely ill-equipped to handle. What would we do, for instance, if Annie's birth mother asked us to help her move to the United States—perhaps even to our home state, New Jersey? Could we really just say no? And if we did, how would Annie view it years from now if she learned that we had turned down her birth mother's request, denying her a chance, maybe her only one, for a better life? Suddenly, my fantasy of finding an intact couple, whose only problem was unemployment, seemed pathetically naive.

As unsettling as I found all these considerations, what upset me the most were the stories of birth mothers who insisted they never meant to give their children up for adoption. A few said they had been coerced into it by family members. One woman said she had been tricked. She had left her baby at the orphanage temporarily, believing she could return when her circumstances improved. She was devastated when she learned that her child had been adopted. Had she signed adoption papers without realizing it? Had the papers been forged? Or had she invented this story out of guilt? There was no way to know.

Soon after, I stumbled across another tragic case in which fraud seemed more than likely. According to the news reports, in 1995, a Russian woman gave birth to a baby who had a disease of the joints; "a monster" was how the doctors described the child. At the grandfather's urging, the doctors told the mother that her child had died. A phony death certificate was drawn up, and the baby was shipped off to an orphanage under a fake name. In 1998, an American couple adopted the child whom they were told no one wanted. A few years later, the birth mother discovered that her baby was alive (and well, thanks to the medical treatment her loving adoptive parents had secured for her). Now she and her husband were waging a battle to get their child back.

We had obtained all the proper documents in our adoption, but could we really be certain that no corruption had been involved? Both of us had been troubled by the large amounts of cash our adoption agency had required us to dole out, without receipts or a detailed accounting of how the money was spent. Where did all that money go, and for what? Certainly not to Annie's orphanage, which had few toys, no playground, no diapers, and only ratty clothes for the kids (though I noticed that the orphanage director had what looked like a new VCR in her office).

One of our motivations for adopting internationally was that we knew these babies needed families. But I wondered what we would do if we learned we had been deceived, and Annie's birth mother had not willingly given up her daughter. The thought of losing Annie was unbearable. I couldn't, wouldn't ever allow that to happen. Yet how could we, or Annie, ever live with the knowledge that Annie was, in effect, stolen from a birth family who had every intention of raising her and loving her?

I reported everything I learned to David, then confided to a few close family members and friends. Everyone's reaction was the same: Don't do it. Too risky. "Let sleeping dogs lie," my brother said.

Instead, I decided to visit an online adoption discussion group. But before I could post a question about whether or not to search, someone else did, prompting a torrent of e-mail—all of it negative. Both adoptive and would-be adoptive parents implored others not to search, arguing that tracking down birth parents was at the very least a violation of the spirit of the law, and could lead to the termination of international adoptions. (This scenario is not as far-fetched as it might sound. As in many other countries, the growing number of adoptions by foreigners, especially Americans, remains a hot-button issue in Kazakhstan; periodically, a politician calls for its cessation.)

Even an adoptee I know, who, as an adult, had looked unsuccessfully for her birth parents, discouraged us from searching. "There are some adult adoptees who would say that it's your daughter's decision to make, not yours," she said. Her friend, also an adoptee, chimed in, telling us about how her birth family had tried to get in touch with her when she was a teenager. It wasn't until almost ten years later that she felt ready.

Then came the question that hit me hard: Do you want to do this search for Annie's sake, or yours?

There was no denying it: I am a habitually curious person. I can't stand the idea of secrets or the unknown. Since adopting Annie, I had thought about her birth parents constantly, why they gave her up, what they looked like, whether they shared Annie's delightful sense of humor, athleticism, or charm. My husband, by contrast, is the type who loves his family and loves them deeply, and that's all he really needs to know. Questions about Annie's birth parents simply don't sprout in his brain unless someone—almost always me—plants them there. "You're obsessed!" David said to me on more than one occasion. And he was right. If I were adopted, I probably would have been one of those people who would not rest until she found her birth parents.

Still, I knew from reading the adoption literature that while many adoptees have a sense of loss and an aching need to know, not all of them feel compelled to find their birth families. How could I possibly know what our happy little two-year-old, who adores her big sister, baby dolls, and the Wiggles, would feel at age twenty? Would Annie take comfort from having the holes in her past filled, and perhaps even have a warm relationship with her birth family (something I dreamed about but knew it was quixotic to wish for)? Or would she resent us for taking away the one decision about adoption that could have been hers to make?

I quietly missed the deadline to join R.'s Kazakhstan search and tried to put it out of my mind.

Almost three months later, David and I had lunch with the adoptive father who had first told me about R., and his family. We already knew that R. had found their child's birth mother and family, and as soon as our kids were comfortably out of earshot, the story poured out of the man and his wife. "It was no Disney family," he told us. "The birth mother was very cold. She didn't seem interested in what happened to her child." He didn't offer details, but the wife later told me that she was so devastated by what they had learned that it took her three days to pick herself up off the floor. Now the couple was struggling with how and when to share the information with their child. Still, they were confident that they had made the right decision. "We have photos, we have a complete medical history, we even know what the grand-parents looked like and what their jobs were," he said. "Our child will have answers. If we waited until he was eighteen, the trail might have gone cold, and it would have been too late."

Not long after, I heard that R. was planning another trip to Kazakhstan in a few months. This time when I told David, he said, "Let's do it." He still didn't have a strong need to know about the birth parents, but he thought Annie might. All that talk of the trail going cold convinced him we had to search. "If we wait, the birth mother could be dead. I just imagine Annie asking us why we didn't try to find her when we had the chance," he said. All of which made per-fect sense—except now I was opposed, petrified that we'd be digging up information that could traumatize Annie, per-haps for life.

Then quite serendipitously, I learned that a woman I had been working with for two years was an adoptee. I had to ask her: Did she think we should search? Her answer was unequivocal: yes. Sharing in an e-mail the story of her decade-long search for her birth family, she urged me to get the facts while we could, store them, and mete them out, telling our daughter what she needs to know when she needs to know it. "Don't assume that she isn't thinking of this whole thing, even while young," she wrote. "I suppressed my desire for years until it became unbearable."

At that moment, I realized that all my months of research, ruminating about everything that could go wrong, had quashed my curiosity. No matter what we learned, I was sure that it would present parenting challenges and moral dilemmas that we probably had no clue how to resolve. *I* no longer wanted to search, but now I was convinced that it was to Annie's ultimate benefit if we did.

In March 2004, we sent R. copies of our documents. A few weeks later, we received his report, complete with photos and a note from the birth mother to Annie. David wept, reading the contents. I felt enormous relief. This was definitely Annie's birth mother—she knew how many weeks early Annie had been born, her birth weight, other details we had been told but had never related to R. My worst fears had not come to pass. The adoption was completely legal. The birth mother, finding herself in dire circumstances, had made an excruciating decision, but undeniably the right one for Annie. She wanted her baby to have a good home. And Annie does.

The rest of the story is for Annie, and only Annie, to know, when she is ready.

Living with a Very
Open Adoption

DAN SAVAGE

There was no guarantee that doing an open adoption would get us a baby any faster than doing a closed or foreign adoption. In fact, our agency warned us that as a gay male couple, we might be in for a long wait. That point was driven home when both birth mothers who spoke at the two-day open adoption seminar we were required to attend said that finding "good, Christian homes" for their babies was their first concern. But we decided to go ahead and do—or try to do—an open adoption anyway. If we became parents, we wanted our child's biological parents to be a part of his life.

As it turns out, we didn't have to wait long. A few weeks after our paperwork was done, we got a call from the agency. A nineteen-year-old homeless street kid named Melissa—

homeless by choice and seven months pregnant by accident—had selected us from the agency's pool of pre-
screened parent wannabes. The day we met Melissa the
agency suggested all three of us go out for lunch—well, all
four of us if you count Wish, Melissa's German shepherd;
all five if you count the baby she was carrying. We were
bursting with touchy-feely questions—which we soon realized was a problem. Stoic and wary, Melissa was only interested in the facts: She was pregnant, didn't want to have an
abortion, and couldn't bring up her baby on the streets.
That left adoption. Even though she hated talking about her
feelings, Melissa was willing to jump through the agency's
hoops—which included weekly counseling sessions and a
few meetings with us—because she wanted to do an
open adoption, too. She wanted, she said, to be a part of her
kid's life.

We were with Melissa when DJ was born. And we were
in her hospital room two days later when it was time for her
to give him up. Before we could take DJ home, before we
could become a family, we literally had to take him from his
mother's arms as she sat sobbing in her bed. It was the hardest thing I've ever done in my life. I was thirty-three years
old when we adopted DJ, and I thought I knew what a broken heart was, how it felt, what it looked like. I didn't know
anything. You know what a broken heart looks like? Like a
sobbing teenager in a hospital bed giving a two-day-old infant
she knows she can't take care of to a couple she hopes can.

Ask a couple hoping to adopt what they want most in
the world and they'll tell you there's only one thing on earth
they want: a baby, a healthy baby. But many couples want

something more: They want their child's biological parents to disappear. They want their child's biological mother and father to be forever absent so there will never be any question about who their child's "real" parents are. The biological parents showing up on their doorstep, lawyers in tow, demanding their kid back, is the collective nightmare of all adoptive parents, endlessly discussed in adoption chat rooms and during adoption seminars.

But we didn't want Melissa to disappear. All adopted kids eventually want to know why they were adopted, and sooner or later they start asking questions. "Why didn't my biological parents keep me?" "Didn't they love me?" "Why did they throw me away?" When kids who were adopted in closed adoptions start asking those questions, there's not a lot the adoptive parents can say. Fact is, they don't know the answers. We would. Having those answers was part of what made doing an open adoption in 1998 seem like the right choice for us.

Like most homeless street kids, Melissa works a national circuit. Portland or Seattle in the summer; Denver, Minneapolis, Chicago, and New York in the late summer and early fall; New Orleans, Phoenix, Las Vegas, or Los Angeles in the winter and spring. Then she hitchhikes or rides the rails back up to Portland, where she's from, and starts all over again. For the first few years after we adopted DJ, Melissa made a point of coming up to Seattle during the summer so we could get together. When she wasn't in Seattle, she kept in touch by phone. Her calls were usually short. She would ask how we're doing, we would ask how she's doing, then we'd put DJ on the phone for a few minutes. She didn't gush, he didn't know what to say. But it was important to DJ that his mother called.

When DJ was three years old, Melissa stopped calling regularly and stopped making a point of coming to town. When she did call, it was usually with disturbing news. One time she called the day after her boyfriend died of alcohol poisoning. They were sleeping on a sidewalk in New Orleans, he was lying beside her, and when she woke up—he was dead. Another time she called after her next boyfriend started using heroin again. Soon the calls stopped, and we began to worry about whether Melissa was alive or dead. After six months with no contact, I started calling hospitals. Then morgues. When the clerk at the county morgue in New Orleans asked me to describe Melissa, without thinking I started to say, "Well, she's kinda quiet . . ." The morgue attendant laughed and told me that all his Jane Does fit that description. When DJ's fourth birthday came and went without a call, I was convinced that something had happened to Melissa on the road or in a train yard somewhere. She had to be dead.

I was tearing down the wallpaper in an extra bedroom at home one night shortly after DJ turned four. His best friend, a little boy named Haven, had spent the night, and after Haven's mother picked him up, DJ dragged a chair into the room and sat down and watched as I pulled wallpaper down in strips. "Haven has a mommy," he suddenly said, "and I have a mommy." DJ was going through a phase where he would make statements of fact and ask us to confirm them for him. It was as if he was testing himself, making sure his take on reality jibed with our own. "That's right," I responded. "You have a mommy, too, just like Haven." He went on. "My mommy's name is Melissa. I came out of my Melissa's tummy. I play with my mommy in the park." Then he looked at me and asked, "When will I see my mommy again?"

"This summer," I said, hoping it wasn't a lie. It was April, and we hadn't heard from Melissa since September of the previous year. "We'll see Melissa in the park, just like last summer."

We didn't see her in the summer. Or the fall or the spring. For a while I wasn't sure what to tell DJ. Suddenly we didn't have the answers anymore. We'd seen her at the hospital, the day she gave him up, and it was the hardest thing I'd ever seen anyone do. We knew that she didn't throw him away, we knew that she loved him. We also knew, though, that Melissa wasn't calling, and for all we knew she was dead. In fact, I was convinced she was dead. But whether she was dead or alive, we weren't sure how to handle the issue of DJ's missing mother. Which two-by-four to hit him with? That his mother was in all likelihood dead? Or that she was out there somewhere but didn't care enough to come by or call? And while we would always be able to tell him how much his mother loved him—we had seen how painful it was for her to give him up—soon he would be asking more complicated questions. What if he wanted to know why his mother didn't love him enough to take care of herself? So she could live long enough to be there for him? So she could tell him herself how much she loved him when he was old enough to remember her and old enough to know what love means?

My partner and I discussed these issues late at night, when DJ was in bed, thankful for each day that passed without the issue of his missing mom coming up. We knew that we wouldn't be able to avoid or finesse the issue of his missing mother after summer arrived in Seattle, something that usually happens in mid-July. As the weeks ticked away, we admitted to each other that those closed adoptions we'd looked down our noses on were starting to look pretty good to us. Instead of being a mystery, DJ's mother was a mass of sometimes very distressing specifics. And instead of dealing with his birth parent's specifics at, say, eighteen or twenty-one, as many adopted children do, he would have to deal with them at four or five.

He was already beginning to deal with them: The last time she visited, when DJ was only three, he wanted to know why his mother smelled so terrible; thankfully, he didn't ask in front of Melissa. We were taken aback by the question and answered it without thinking it through. We explained that since she's homeless, she isn't able to bathe often or wash her clothes ever. We realized we screwed up even before DJ started to freak. What, after all, could be more terrifying to a child than the idea of not having a home? Telling him that his mother chooses to live on the streets, that for her the streets were home, didn't cut it. For months DJ insisted that his mother was just going to have to come and live with us. We had a bathroom, we had a washing machine. She could sleep in the guest bedroom.

When Grandma came to visit, she could sleep in his bed and he would sleep on the floor.

I don't recommend that anyone trying to talk a reluctant partner into doing an open adoption let them read the rest of this essay.

We did hear from Melissa again, fourteen months later, when she called from Portland, Oregon. She wasn't dead, only thoughtless. She had just kind of lost track of time, she explained, and didn't make it up to Seattle before it got too cold and wet, and whenever she thought about calling it was either too late or she was too drunk. When she told me that she'd reached the point where she got sick when she didn't drink, I gently suggested that maybe it was time to get off the streets, stop drinking and using drugs, and think about her future. I could hear her rolling her eyes. The reason she'd chosen us over all the straight couples she could've chosen was that we didn't look old enough to be her parents. We looked like we could be her peers. She didn't want us to start acting like her parents, she said. She didn't want to be lectured. She would get off the streets when she was ready. She wasn't angry, she didn't raise her voice. She just wanted to make sure we understood each other.

During this conversation, the first one in which we ever broached the subject of her, for lack of a better word, "lifestyle," Melissa was calm, cool, and rational. Despite the fact that she continues to make the same choices, all the while expecting a different outcome—one popular definition of insanity—I don't think Melissa is mentally ill. She's built a life for herself that allows her to avoid taking responsibility or confronting the pain of what I gather was a pretty shitty childhood. Why should she get off the streets? She's proud, she tells us, that she lives on the streets so successfully, deceased boyfriends notwithstanding. It's something she does well, she says. It's her thing.

DJ was happy to hear from his mother, and the fourteen months without a call or a visit were forgotten. We went down to Portland to see her, she apologized to DJ in person, we took some pictures, and she promised not to disappear again.

We didn't hear from her for a year. This time she wasn't drunk. She was in prison, charged with assault. She'd been in prison before, for short stretches, picked up on vagrancy and trespassing charges. But this time was different. This time she needed our help. Or her dog did. Suddenly she wanted us to start acting like her parents.

Not much had changed in the six years between our first meeting and that phone call from prison. Melissa had lost a few boyfriends to drugs and alcohol; she'd made the awkward transition from street kid to homeless person. But besides aging—and living on the streets ages you pretty fast—very little about Melissa's life had changed. Wake up, beg for change, buy food for her dog and alcohol for herself and her friends, hang out, talk, avoid the cops, move on. But while her life hadn't changed, the people in her life had. The other homeless kids she traveled around with were constantly disappearing, her boyfriends had a bad habit of dying, vanishing, or getting put away. Her dog Wish, however, was the one constant presence in her life. She lived for Wish and Wish lived for her. Having a large dog complicates hitchhiking and hopping trains, of course, but Melissa is a petite woman and her dog offers her some protection. And love. And constancy.

Late one night in New Orleans, she told us from a noisy common room, she got into an argument with another homeless person. He lunged at her in a threatening way, Melissa said, and Wish bit him. New Orleans is a city where the police are under orders to treat as roughly as possible the homeless kids who pester the drunk tourists for their spare change. Melissa had once been ticketed for being drunk in public in New Orleans—on Bourbon Street, of all places, where absolutely everyone is drunk and the sidewalks reek of vomit no matter how many times they hose them down. She was calling, she said, because it didn't look as though she was going to get out of prison before the pound would put Wish down. She was distraught. We had to help her, she begged, we had to save Wish. She was crying, the first time I'd heard her cry since that day in the hospital six years ago. Five weeks and $1,600 later, we had managed not only to save Wish but also to get Melissa out and the charges dropped. When we talked on the phone, I urged her to get out of New Orleans. I found out three months later that she'd taken my advice—she was calling from a jail in Virginia, where she'd been arrested for trespassing at a train yard. Wish was okay, he was with friends, she was only calling to say hello to DJ.

I've heard people say that choosing to live on the streets is a kind of slow-motion suicide. Having known Melissa for six years now, I'd say that's accurate. Everywhere she goes, everything she does, she seems to court danger. I've lost track of the number of friends and boyfriends she's told me about who have died of overdoses, alcohol poisoning, and hypothermia. As he gets older, DJ is getting a more accurate picture of his mother, but so far it doesn't seem to be an issue for him. He loves her. A photo of a family reunion we attended isn't complete, he insists, because his mother isn't in it. He wants to see her this summer, "even if she smells," he says. We're looking forward to seeing her, too. But I'm tired.

Now for the may-God-rip-off-my-fingers-before-I-type-this part of the essay: I'm starting to get anxious for Melissa's slow-mo suicide to end, whatever that end looks like. I'd prefer that it end with Melissa off the streets, in an apartment somewhere, pulling her life together, but as she gets older that resolution is getting harder and harder to picture.

A lot of people who self-destruct don't think twice about destroying their children in the process. Maybe Melissa knew she was going to self-destruct and loved DJ so much that she wanted to make sure he wouldn't get hurt. She left him somewhere safe, with parents she chose for him, even though it broke her heart to give him away, because she knew that if he was close she would hurt him, too. Sometimes I wonder if this answer will be good enough for DJ when he asks us why his mother couldn't hold it together just enough to stay in the world for him. I kind of doubt it.

Two Daughters,
Two Destinies

LAURA SHAINE CUNNINGHAM

I imagined the three of us on an astounding odyssey, "Around the World on Our Personal Adoption Tour." My dream for our next summer vacation was to take my two daughters, now thirteen and eleven, to see their birthplaces in Transylvania, Romania, and China. In my fantasy, we three would visit the tiny village where Alexandra was born in the Carpathian Mountains, then whisk off (perhaps on the Trans-Siberian Express?) to Shanghai, where I found Jasmine in the Children's Welfare Institute. For me, the proposed journey was a mix of adventure and maternal déjà vu—a fantasy that fizzled this New Year's Eve when I proposed the trip to the girls and found that both were reluctant to go.

Jasmine refused to return to China. Alexandra was less adamant but showed no enthusiasm. I was stunned and disappointed, but hesitated to push on them a journey so laden with significance. The trip would succeed only if we were all in tune. My own history as an orphan and an adopted child made me wary of insisting or even urging.

I knew that we were treading on delicate ground, since my two daughters had such disparate backgrounds. For one child, I had a portfolio of family photos, detailed descriptions, and addresses. For the other, I had the standard orphan's document—a name, a date, and saddest of all, a street address where the baby had been left.

Not only the inequity of their stories but my own private history as a baby born out of wedlock, orphaned, and later adopted myself made my heartbeat quicken and my voice tighten when I asked each girl in turn for her reasons. Why did they not show curiosity, even eagerness, to view the country and culture into which they had been born? If anything, their father (now my ex-husband) and I have steered hard in the opposite direction with Chinese and Romanian friends, groups, and language classes. They knew and loved friends from their birth countries. I extolled the foreign cultures, and I myself could not have been more eager to return to my daughters' birthplaces.

I had been orphaned at eight, the daughter of a single mother named Rosie who died too young. There seemed no likely candidate to "raise" me, an only child, now parentless. My father had been a mystery, an alleged hero who never returned from a fictitious war. In those long-ago preliberation days, respectable women did not bear babies out of wedlock—especially not thirty-five-year-old "career" women like my mother, who was from an educated middle-class family.

My own mother died with the secret of my paternity, and her wedding band that she had bought herself. She had made a weak attempt to pass as a "war widow," a thin ruse that never worked, as the country was not at war. She gave me an overexposed photo of my father—his image so faint he almost disappeared from the picture, as he had from my life—then filled in the blanks. I was named Laura, for "Larry," the love of her life. He was the handsomest man she ever knew; he was the best dancer. He could fly a plane better than anyone else—a handy part of the legend, as he did in fact fly away. When I was five, my mother said his plane crashed, and he would never return to us. Parts of her story were so fanciful—he flew a plane with a trained dog as his copilot—that it was not long before I realized the truth. I knew little that could be verified about my father. He was a fiction. "Did he see me before he left?" was my most insistent question as a child. "Did he see me before he left?" had no verifiable answer.

Before my mother went into the hospital, Rosie delegated her "kid" brother to look after me in what she believed would be a two-week absence. When she never returned home, my Uncle Gabe, thirty-eight, was joined by his older brother, Len, forty, who was also a bachelor; the two unmarried men thought it best to raise me together. My uncles were adoring and adored. I grew up inclined toward the concept of families being created, not necessarily "born." I also grew up with two adoptive fathers, but also an inheritance—of missing facts and missing people.

Although I had married at nineteen, my husband and I postponed parenthood. We waited too long. At forty-two,

I had tried, I admit ambivalently, to conceive. It took me about one second to look toward adoption. In my heart, I think I wanted a baby or child, already born, whose fate I could understand.

My journey, the one I wished to reprise with my daughters, began in late summer 1990, when my husband and I flew to Romania. Even now, as I consider the twin return trips, I realize the visits cannot be in any way identical. Would the differences hurt my daughters? Injure one daughter and "reward" the other? Would it be fair to return to one country and not the other? Should I try to persuade the girls to embark on journeys that would give each a separate and unequal truth? I had to weigh the circumstances to decide how to proceed; I had to review each story to see what merit each girl might find at her birthplace.

In a cinderblock Soviet-style hospital in the Carpathian Mountains of Transylvania, Romania, I fell in love with my first daughter. Alexandra entered, squalling, her face a tomato under a mop of Eskimo-black bangs. She was three days old.

The birth mother was a shy, dark-haired young woman of twenty-three, who, from her hospital bed, kissed me on both cheeks. The translator reported that she felt we had "saved" her baby from going to the orphanage down the road. I could not know then what I do now—that only my first daughter would have the legacy of a birth family and a known history. Alexandra's birth family was still in attendance (save the father, who was said to have gone far up into the mountains and had not, in fact, married the mother). The birth mother had already had a baby the year before; she was one of the victims of policies that allowed no birth control, no abortion.

My husband and I were invited to her parents' homestead in the fourteen-family village. We saw the compound with its scrubbed cottage and outdoor cooking fires. The grandmother had wall-sized cupboards lined with tapestries; the women of their family had woven for many generations. The grandfather showed us his hundreds of sheep and a single pony. Most poignantly, we saw the boy who was less than two years older than Alexandra, a beautiful child, whom the grandparents had now chosen to adopt. They were shepherds, it was explained, and the boy could work in the mountains, leading the flocks. The grandparents, so warm toward us, could not accept this second baby born out of wedlock. The girl, now our beloved, was not to be kept.

Yet many members of the birth family seemed loving and warm toward the baby. I stored the memories to share with Alexandra—the warm hospitality, the planned feast, the kindness of her young aunt and uncle, only in their twenties, who had sought out adoptive parents for her. In a winsome twist, this young aunt was giving birth herself the very next day. As I visited the nursery, I saw the beautiful twenty-one-year-old aunt walk to the labor room. Within hours, another baby, her new son, was snug in his bunting, next to Alexandra, the first cousin he might never know.

I took many photographs of this family, pictures I have shared with Alexandra. Having been the child of a mystery father, I gleaned some precious facts about her birth father's name, the fact that he was "the tallest, handsomest man" in the village, and, as the birth mother shyly related, "He had a mustache." Her smile told me more, as my own mother's smile had told me; she had loved the father. I wondered how Alexandra would react when the legend came to life. I believed that most of her birth family would embrace her. But would this other disparity—the boy babies kept at home—hurt my daughter in ways I could not even imagine? Could her birth mother give her what I hoped, love in some nonconfusing form? Or would tears of regret, or some unpredictable response, mar the reunion?

I began to feel a bit skittish. All adopted children had fantasies of their absent parents. I had many times envisioned reunion and embrace that for me had never occurred. What if she were welcomed so warmly that everyone wished her to stay? Or what if she found no welcome but experienced something I myself had always dreaded—a rejection?

For a time, I had exchanged notes with the family. I even sent them photographs of the blooming brunette baby. But their letters were in an almost indecipherable English, and faded away. It had been years since we had had contact. Yet I believed there was more good than pain to come from Alexandra's return.

Could I anticipate the same possibility for Jasmine, whose background would be a blank? It was a very different morning on which I met my second child in December 1992. There were omens galore that this second adoption had a foreshadowed sense of danger. My husband and I had flown off in a blizzard heralded as "The Storm of the Century." And the storm raged in the airplane as well. Seated in the mock domesticity of the cabin, side by side, we were barely speaking. Our twenty-six-year marriage was strained at the seams. I had a premonition then that everything would be more difficult on this second journey.

Now, as I remember the shivery flight and our descent into darkness on that Shanghai night, even I wonder, Should I take my daughter Jasmine back to a place where her origin was listed as "left on Quon Dong Road"? What will she find there, at the orphanage?

What we found was a place so cold that we wore our hats and coats indoors and the nurses held steaming mugs of green tea. They did not wish to uncover the baby's face—"Too cold." Baby Jasmine Sou Mei was swaddled in old comforters that were unwrapped to reveal her chafed and bleeding bottom. Wheezing and ill, she could not cry; she had no strength. She clung to me, a piteous elf, with stick-out ears, and huge, sad eyes. Her mouth tugged downward, in the melancholy expression I saw on so many orphanage babies. Jasmine Sou Mei's papers, rather than the list of relatives I had on Alexandra's, show no parents' names, only that chilling street address where she was found, "Quon Dong Road." Even then, I wondered how I would later tell Jasmine that I knew nothing about her family history. It was so different from the fat memory book and smiling photos of her "other" family that two-year-old Alexandra possessed.

There followed miracles and calamity. My daughters adored each other. Alexandra was the most maternal of big sisters. Jasmine called for "Bissy," Big Sister, as soon as she could call for me. I was so happy as a mother; it was almost tragic to admit my marriage had failed, almost instantly, upon the second adoption. My husband and I had both wanted both daughters, but the warmth in our marriage had chilled. Divorce was inevitable.

So the girls inherited different households as well. Alexandra knew three years at home with a mother and father; Jasmine was the baby of divorce, who would never have a memory of her adoptive parents as a couple. The divorce was a ragged, painful business. The love between me and my little girls, the three-way orbit, sustained us. There was a day I would never forget. I staggered in, drained by the ordeal, and placed the baby on the sofa, knowing I would need to change her diaper, and to my surprise, turned and found that in the blink of an eye, three-year-old Alexandra had used a baby wipe on her baby sister's bottom, tidily taped on the new diaper, sealed the old, and disposed of it in the diaper pail. Gradually, the serrated edge of divorce became less cutting. Their father has alternate weekends, and some vacation time. He, too, shares the dream of their rediscovering their heritages.

For Jasmine, I constructed a photo album, but I knew it could not match Alexandra's. In fact, it was a study in contrasts. Alexandra is shown with her birth family. Jasmine is depicted in a green crib in the Shanghai orphanage, the only supporting cast the staff of the orphanage. The Chinese doctor and the nursing and paralegal staff are all aglow; their smiles light the album. But can they compare with the family that beams in Alexandra's memory book? How can I show Jasmine an institute, after escorting Alexandra to a mountain village with ponies and lambs, peopled by warm and eager blood relatives?

Yet as an adopted child myself, I swear by the truth. Lies and evasion, I feel, do harm. The truth, gently told, would be freeing. Seeing would be believing. How could anyone resist an exotic country of origin? An insight into her own genetic past?

Today, I do what every mother of more than one child does—I try to divvy the goods, in equal gifts, to both girls. Their legacies, I feel, are sacred offerings. For Jasmine, I emphasize her culture, her own style, which is inherently Chinese. This winter, we attended a Chinese brush painting course, and her delicate strokes evoked more than the rice paper images of bamboo. I would take her to China, I imagined, to show her the source, the paintings, the terracotta warriors, the Great Wall, the wonders. But will she ever want to go?

While Alexandra, who shares my Eastern European background, looks startlingly like me, Jasmine resembles me in her obsession to write. Like me, she writes tales of "orphans," paupers who become princesses. She is a joyous girl, but her questions began, if only tentatively. "Why did you choose me? Were the other babies ugly?"

"I chose you because I fell in love with you when you turned your head and looked into my eyes," I tell her. "I saw your soul, and knew you were my daughter."

She smiles each time I say this.

Alexandra is shy about her memory book. While she does not choose to expand conversation with me, or her sister, regarding the birth family, I did overhear her explaining her "other" family to a friend. One day, she took copies of her photos to school. I have heard her say, "I have a brother." A friend gave her the national flag of Romania; she keeps it, I think tellingly, beside her bed. During the 2004 Summer Olympics in Athens, she took pride in watching a Romanian gymnast with her name distinguish herself in competition.

Seizing such clues, I again, several months after my initial New Year's proposal, offer both girls the opportunity to journey to their birthplaces. As a young child, Alexandra seemed faintly intrigued by and proud of Romania. She would often say, "The Romanians are the best." Then, abruptly, she clammed up regarding matters Romanian. She does not want to go there, she tells me now. "I don't want to see the sheep," she says. But what of the birth mother, the grandparents, her charming aunt and uncle, and same-age cousin? The big brother who was last seen playing a toy balalaika? "I might like to see the brother someday," she admits. But not now.

If it were I, I could not resist the lure of that second, unknown family. I would want to see everyone; find my new place, not to remain but to revisit. But Alexandra seems unmovable. She says that she has a mother and father. Here. I will not force this; if she fears this journey, it must not happen.

Jasmine was always and remains adamant. "Don't take me to China. They were not nice to me there." As Jasmine was only ten weeks old when she departed, I could never solve this mystery of how she could know she was in such poor condition in the orphanage. I had never told her of the cold rags on her body; the chafed skin; her sad eyes and piteous wailings. To compensate, I injected more Chinese culture into her life. We have Chinese-born and Chinese-American friends; she studies Chinese language. She has even attended a Chinese church. Her father dated Chinese women.

"I'm American," Jazzy insists.

"But I love Chinese culture; I can't wait to return," I tell her.

She looks doubtful.

In our bedtime talk, I again ask the girls why they do not share my dream of a return to their birthplaces. "We like it here," they say, in unison. I recall that my own curiosity and yearning for my father did not really surface until I was sixteen. Then the urge kicked in with a vengeance. I traveled south to find him, and failed. No trace. And no clues. I closed the book, empty, on my own father. I have heard that it is not unusual for adolescence to spark this obsession to retrieve the beginning.

This past year, I had to travel, on business, to Russia, home of my grandparents. Alexandra elected not to accompany me, but to my surprise, Jasmine insisted she not be left behind. To my delight, Jasmine was a thrilled and thrilling companion. I can't imagine we won't all somehow travel again.

Jazzy still rhapsodizes about the palaces of St. Petersburg, the flight with exotic delicacies from Finland, and, best of all, she says, the hotel bathroom, with its marble tub. She can't wait to return—to Russia. Our travels inspired a question: "Could the hotel in China be as nice?" I can answer truthfully to my eleven-year-old, "The Chinese hotel was even nicer."

Then, as gently as I can, I segue to the fact of the orphanage and what she might find there, if she chose to go. I recall the courtyard with its red tiled roof, and bamboo, the line of rag diapers drying in the sun.

"We can bring them better diapers," Jasmine suggests. "Lots of diapers."

I look at her—stunned. The marble tub I understood but the diapers? Altruism at eleven?

"Yes," she says. "Let's bring them the diapers, but don't expect me to put them on the babies."

I cannot help but laugh. The maternal Alexandra now looks very interested—in going to China. Somehow, my Round the World has become a roller coaster, of upside-down surprises, but I can smile and look toward a future adventure that I now believe will happen—perhaps in some eccentric manner, out of sequence.

Someday, I hope the girls will both feel secure enough to trust me to take them (round-trip) to their native lands, knowing that we will return home. Until then, we live, as they say, in our moments. A mother and two daughters, not so different after all.

♥

TWO

Encounters with the Unexpected

Post-Adoption Panic

MELISSA FAY GREENE

When I found myself weeping in the laundry room over being forced to put my children's sheets on the interloper's bed (because, at age four and a half, he was wetting the bed), I knew I was in trouble.

Refusing to take photos of him during his first weeks in America (because it might mean he was staying, because the photos might be used as evidence that he'd been here) also might have been a clue. Refusing to let anyone else take a picture of the whole family (because his presence in the family portrait among our four kids by birth would mar the effect) similarly could have sounded a warning note.

Ditto my wondering what would happen if he rolled over in the night and somehow fell out a second-story window onto the driveway.

And there was the day, in the grocery store checkout line, when a cashier brightly asked, "Would you like to contribute a dollar for Thanksgiving dinners for the homeless?" and I snarled, with murderous anger, "I . . . HAVE . . . GIVEN . . . ENOUGH."

Lying awake at night considering, "If I leave right now, drive all night, and check into a motel in Indiana, will anyone ever find me?" also might have signaled that I was having some issues with our son, whom we had just adopted from Bulgaria in October 1999.

My husband knew. I couldn't stop myself from shaking him awake at night to sob and complain. I insisted, in the small hours of the morning, that he agree with me that we'd spoiled our lives and the lives of our children, then ages seven, eleven, fourteen, and seventeen. "It just doesn't feel like when we brought the *other* kids home from the hospital," I said, weeping.

Don, a bearded defense attorney, answered softly, with some surprise, "To me it does." I turned away from him and let the ridiculous man go back to sleep. All night long I thrashed and pummeled my pillow, in the grip of panic and grief and regret.

One night, trying desperately to pull myself together, I woke up Don and announced, "Okay, I've figured something out: If I think about my friends, I realize that many of them are facing really difficult issues. This one is in the middle of an awful divorce, that one is fighting breast cancer, this one just lost her job." I waited for his assent.

"Wow," Don said mildly. "Well, yes . . . but this was supposed to be a *happy* thing."

One morning, I pulled a telephone as far as it would reach from one room to the privacy of another, dialed the long-distance phone number of the adoption agency, and whispered, "I don't think I can do this. Is it possible to disrupt an adoption?"

"Well, gosh," chirruped a friendly voice on the other end. "Nobody's ever asked me that before! Let me find somebody to ask."

Undone to learn that I was the first, the very first, adoptive mother to even ask such a question, I was incapable of gathering enough voice to reply. I hung up on the woman and doubled over in agony.

"Can you believe I've done this to myself?" I cried to a visiting friend, gesturing wildly at the child. Jesse, with his neat brown bangs and dark eyes, was sitting at that moment on the screened porch, with his legs straight out in front of him, trying to learn how to play with blocks. He looked up from the blocks often to make sure I was nearby, to seek my approval for his block-touching. He'd never had anything to play with in the orphanage. So far that morning he'd confirmed that the wood blocks were not edible, but he was unsure what he was supposed to do next. I was in too foul a mood to show him.

"Can you remember why you *wanted* to adopt?" asked my friend, at a loss as to how to help me. The child looked fine to her; he looked cute, even.

"No!" I sobbed. "I can't! It was another person; it wasn't me. I can't even remember that person. What was she thinking?"

I knew what she had been thinking: she had been thinking, "Our children are so wonderful, our house is so full of love, we're good parents. Let's bring in another little kid from somewhere and prolong the fun."

Ha ha. What a mistake. Instead of prolonging the fun

with our four children, I now grasped, I'd never see them again. Every time I tried to spend a moment alone with one of them, Jesse came barreling into the room and threw himself onto my body. He was thrilled to have been given a mother, even a rumpled, disconsolate one like myself. He pulled me into the bathroom with him, insisting I wait. He wanted me to watch him eat. He couldn't fall asleep unless I was sitting on his bed. Whenever I disappeared from his line of vision, he went berserk, falling to the floor in a fit, screaming and thrashing. This was happening four or five times a day. When I slipped outside to walk my seven-year-old daughter, Lily, to school one morning, as I'd always done in our former life, the little boy screamed his outrage in the front hall and then tried to run through the glass storm door to stop me. Somehow Lily's hand got caught by the storm door. She and I ran away crying up the hill to school. "I said he could come," she wailed, "but I didn't know he was going to hurt me." We staggered on toward school, blinded by unhappiness. After I dropped her off, I could barely drag myself home. A friend spotted me on the sidewalk and pulled over. Though my spirits lifted ever so faintly when she picked me up, I crashed again when we pulled into my driveway thirty seconds later. I had hoped we were going somewhere new. Like to Europe.

The landscape flattened. I drove slowly through my neighborhood, heartsick at how the houses and yards had become two-dimensional, like comic-strip sketches, almost colorless. I recognized everything, but I could no longer insert myself into the scene. It had become shrink-wrapped when I was outside of it. I was closed out forever.

I drove through Atlanta, weeping, with Jesse buckled in the backseat. I tuned in to every moment of the NPR station's fall fund-raiser, listening not for the classical music but for the studio chatter. I listened in the car, then I ran in and turned on the radio in the kitchen. I felt so frighteningly alone that the fund-raising pitches felt like conversation to me, the voices felt like company.

My sudden bizarre fervor for adoption, I now believed, had ruined what was most precious to me on earth: my family. "Post-adoption depression" never crossed my mind. I hadn't yet put my hands on the little research that had been done on the subject. So I didn't know that it was quite common among adoptive mothers of older postinstitutionalized children. The reasons vary. But surely it is in part because adults are hard-wired to attach to wide-eyed, helpless babies; a fit-throwing, non-English-speaking, snarling Bulgarian four-year-old does not, at first glimpse, invite adoration. The crucial early period of tender mother-infant courtship is missed as sorely by adult women as it is missed by the older orphanage kids who suddenly parachute into their lives with their boots on.

In the orphanage in rural Bulgaria, the director had taken the little boy by the shoulders, turned him to face me, and said, "Mama," and that was it for Jesse—a light went on in his mind, an archetypal image was personified: "Mama." He felt instantly devoted to me, instantly cared for. Jesse was not having "bonding" or "attachment" issues, as can happen with older-child adoption. But I was.

Adoption agency websites and brochures, magazine articles and adoption memoirs brimmed with "love at first sight" epiphanies. Some mothers reported falling in love the minute they met their children; others, when they saw a video; still others, when they beheld a blurry black-and-white faxed photograph. None of that happened to me. I hadn't been visited by "love at first sight" and I couldn't figure out where the love was going to come from, or how on earth I would survive the coming years of raising the boy. I was reeling with the sudden tremendous and terrible revelation that if you don't love a child, there's no way on earth you can bend to the hundred daily subservient tasks of caring for him. All the little things I'd done thousands of times for my older children were impossible to perform for a child I didn't love. He was like the sleepover friend who overstays his welcome. "*When* is that family going to pick this child *up?*" one felt.

It wasn't until the afternoon in the laundry room, awash in a feeling of pity for our old sheets, that I first thought: "You're crying over sheets. You're losing it."

Followed by: "You'd better get help."

Followed by: "If you succeed in convincing your husband that your lives are ruined, you'll never get out of this spot. There will be no one left to pull you out."

I made a doctor's appointment. "Today. I need to see her *today.*"

"Can you come tomorrow afternoon?"

"I think so," I said in a tiny voice.

"People take something for this, don't they? Aren't there drugs for this kind of thing?" I asked the physician the next afternoon.

"You're completely exhausted," she said. "Are you sleeping?"

"No."

"Are you eating?"

"No."

"Have you caught up on your sleep since the jet lag of flying back from Bulgaria?"

Though I'd been back three weeks now, I still hadn't.

"I'm going to give you something to help you sleep," she said.

I burst into tears. "I need something stronger! I'm crying over *sheets.*"

"Okay, okay," she said. The doctor, who had known me for fifteen years, had never seen me like this. She brought me some sort of pharmaceutical sample. I grabbed it. In my car in the parking lot, I snapped open the package and swallowed the tablet whole, dry, without water. Instantly I began to feel better. I didn't care that the instructions said to allow six weeks for the medication to take effect; the placebo effect pulled me back from the brink.

There were other things I did right: I told my friends I was in bad shape. I'd never reached out for help from such a scared and vulnerable place before, and my good friends flew to my side. They sat with me. They helped me watch Jesse. I couldn't be alone with him. It wasn't that *he* had a behavior problem; *I* did. When I found myself alone with him, I sank into despair.

My friends also gave good advice. "You don't have to love him," one said consolingly over coffee. "You can just pretend to love him. He won't know. Jesse's never been so mothered in his life. Jesse's in heaven. Just fake it. Your faking it is the greatest, sweetest thing that's ever happened to him."

While faking it, while pretending to love him, I discovered that my body was okay with mothering him—my lips knew how to kiss him, my hands enjoyed stroking his hair. Yes, my heart was in total rebellion, my brain frozen with regret, but I tried to lose the panic for a little while and just follow the willingness of my body to mother him.

"Do you love him yet?"

Such an awful thing we adoptive parents do to ourselves and our newly adopted children, asking ourselves this question. "Do you love her yet?" Like the television ads for Cingular wireless phones: "Can you hear me now?" "Do you love him now?" We don't pursue this line of questioning about the children to whom we gave birth. Even when our oldest child, at sixteen, broke curfew and gave a lift to an entire punk-rock band, too many for her seat belts, my husband and I never asked ourselves, "Do we love her?" We loved her more than the sun, moon, and stars; we just didn't want her driving around at 3 A.M. in strange parts of Atlanta with six members of a punk band.

Yet here sat this little guy at the table, painstakingly peeling a hot dog before eating it, looking up with his shaggy haircut and sparkly eyes, and all I could think was: "Do I love him yet?"

Well, he loved me, and that little steady unwavering beacon of love began to lure me.

One night, within the first month of Jesse's arrival, sleepless again, I strayed from my bedroom and ended up resting on the daybed in my downstairs office. In the middle of the night, Jesse, also a night wanderer, found me. I opened the covers and he climbed in beside me. "Damn!

He found me! Damn!" I felt trapped and angry. Yet I was not insensitive to the sensation of the little boy curling and purring beside me; he nuzzled and snuggled like a kitten. At first light, I sprang out of bed to put distance between us; when he got up, he found me in the kitchen and drew me by the hand back to the office. He pointed to the bed and said, in baby-Bulgarian-English, "Mama speesh; Cha-chee speesh." ("Mama sleep, Jesse sleep.") All day long, he remembered, and reminded me, laughing: "Mama speesh, Cha-chee speesh," pointing to himself to help me remember our great encounter, our wonderful secret. That night he tried to make it happen again, but I stayed in my own bedroom, with the door closed. I heard him looking for me downstairs.

He was intoxicated with everything I did. One night, as I dressed to go out somewhere, he sat high on my bed, swinging his legs, watching me. On went the stockings, on went the slip, on went the low heels; before I could finish buttoning the satin blouse, Jesse flew off the bed and into the closet to hug me. "Oh, *Mama!*" he cried, utterly starstruck. He adored picking through my jewelry box to find pairs of earrings, and took very seriously the responsibility of choosing a set for me to wear. It was like he'd been starved not only for a mama, but for all the accoutrements of a mama.

Under such an onslaught of tenderness, I began to soften.

I no longer assumed he was leaving; I assumed he was staying. He no longer assumed I was leaving; he began to trust that I was staying. He began to let me out of his sight for minutes on end. I was able to walk Lily to school in the morning, savoring every step, every breath of the fall air, like heaven had been restored to me. I was able to listen to my older daughter practice her upright bass, and to my older son play his trombone, seated on the beds in their rooms without a small Bulgarian draped across me. Lily discovered that Jesse would let her dress him up like a big doll. She decked him out in beads and wigs and ballerina tutus and karate belts, and led him into the living room so all of us could laugh and clap. When he became enamored of the cartoon hero Hercules, and insisted on wearing a cape at all times, Lily helped him find just the right cape and arranged it across his shoulders. He began to follow Lily around devotedly.

One afternoon, feeling irascible and weary, I gave in to his pleas of "Bagel, Mama? Bagel? Bagel?" and hacked so hard at a stale bagel that the knife glanced off the roll and slashed my finger. I ran upstairs to get cotton to stop the bleeding. Jesse followed in a panic. "Mama! Oh, Mama! Mama!" His eyes were huge and filled with tears. He stood beside me as I sat on the closed toilet trying to stanch the bleeding; he patted and patted my shoulder. "Mama!" he announced. "Mama, nay bagel, Mama, nay bagel." He was trying to help after the fact by unrequesting the bagel.

Downstairs, later, he stood on his tiptoes, reached into the kitchen drawer, extracted the big guilty knife, and said, "Nay Mama this. *Daddy*. Nay Mama. *Daddy*." Meaning you should not use this knife anymore; let Daddy use it.

Still later he had an updated announcement to make. He dashed into the kitchen, pointed to the knife, and said,

"Nay Mama, nay Franny." (The rat terrier.) "Daddy." I know he loved the dog very much already; I don't know if this policy statement was meant to protect the two individuals he most loved from the bad knife, or if he now put me in the competence department with the dog.

Finally, toward the end of the day, he came to me with a plastic picnic knife he'd found somewhere. He put it in my bandaged hand and said, firmly, "Mama."

What was it I felt at that moment, as I laughed and wept and accepted the picnic knife and hugged him? Was it, actually . . . could it be . . . ? Well, by then I was trying hard to stop grilling myself a dozen times daily: "Do you love him yet?" I had learned about postadoption depression and realized such interrogation was getting me nowhere.

But if this wasn't the beginning of an old-fashioned sweet mother-son relationship, this repentant little boy handing me, so earnestly, a plastic knife, I didn't know what was.

I had an appointment with a psychologist scheduled for a few days after the bagel mishap. But after Jesse handed me that plastic knife, I phoned ahead to cancel it, and scheduled a haircut instead. I took him with me. If he thought I was beautiful before the haircut, he *really* thought I was beautiful after the haircut. He thought the whole haircut experience was a glamorous and magnificent and elegant thing, full of the scents of perfumes and hairsprays and peppermints in a dish. I glanced back at him in the backseat, his cheek big with a peppermint, as I drove home. He gave me a huge sticky smile. Did I love him? I didn't ask.

Baby on Board—but Not Everyone Else

SHEILA STAINBACK

My family is one of those huge, sprawling clans that leave visitors saying, Now, tell me again, that one is *whose* child? As the fourth of six siblings, I have fifteen nieces and nephews, who at last count had fifteen children among them. When my younger sister Roslyn sends out her quarterly newsletter, which lovingly updates family milestones, with an emphasis on the youngest members of the tribe, it goes to twenty-five addresses, most of them in the New York area. Between editions of the family newsletter, we get together regularly: Christmas, Thanksgiving, and since my father's death in 1998 (with its attendant reminder that our time together is short), other holidays, too, especially my mother's birthday. As you can imagine, those family gatherings, mostly at my mother's apartment on Manhattan's Lower East Side, can be a bit chaotic and raucous, with the adults taking stock of how their various nieces and nephews have grown.

Given all that, you would think that bringing another child into the fold would be no big deal. Okay, maybe I had a few reservations about it. A single journalist in my late forties, I had never shared with my family my plan to adopt. And I had heard those horror stories about families that shun an adopted child. But I figured that we are, if nothing else, an elastic bunch, built to expand and absorb. So in the spring of 2001, it was with a mix of excitement and apprehension that I told first my mother, then each of my five siblings, that I was about to adopt Charles, an energetic boy who had spent his first two and a half years in the city's foster care system.

Initially, everyone reacted just as I had hoped. My mother and siblings all congratulated me and told me that I'd be a great mom. No one seemed concerned that motherhood would arrive for me by way of adoption. Being a single mother wasn't an issue at all, given that several of my nieces are single moms. I came away relieved and convinced that my family wasn't going to be one of those more fixated on where the child came from than who the child was.

But then the grumbling started. "Why is Sheila adopting a stranger's child, when we have all these kids in the family who can use her help?" my older sister Dorothy said to my mom. When that remark accidentally found its way to me, it stung. Among my siblings, Dorothy, the mother of most of my nieces and nephews (nine to be exact), is the closest to me in age. Though in childhood we'd shared a rough-and-tumble rivalry, over the years we had grown so close that I regarded her as the most loving and supportive of my siblings. If Dorothy could talk this way behind my back, what about my other family members? Was the encouragement I received from them also false? Was my family—the one that would soon become Charles's as well—one of those dreaded families I'd heard about that consigns adopted children to the status of outsider?

I decided to let the remark pass. I wanted to be optimistic. As a nervous mother-to-be, I not only yearned for my family's approval and support, I suspected that I'd need them. I had read all the statistics and studies. Charles fit the standard profile of the majority of children in the New York City foster care system: minority, male, possibly exposed to drugs in utero. But I knew that whoever I adopted from the foster care system would in some way have "special needs." This fact did not worry me especially. A few of my nieces and nephews had required early intervention for developmental delays, or been consigned to special education classes. They'd turned out fine. Given my training as a reporter, I was confident that I could fight for and secure whatever special services Charles might need to thrive. Still, let's face it: having backup helps.

I also felt that history was on my side. For generations in America, black families like mine have taken in children who were not biologically theirs. In earlier decades, the relationship was often informal, involving neither the exchange of documents nor government oversight. (It also seldom involved any hint to the child of his or her biological origins.) These "promised children," as Nicholas Lemann wrote in his 1992 book *The Promised Land,* were typically turned over to infertile women by birth mothers who unexpectedly had found themselves pregnant or perhaps with one child too many. The crack cocaine epidemic of the 1980s and '90s ushered in a new consideration: children born to drug-addicted parents, who were neglected or simply abandoned. Although these children were not believed to have much "promise," because of their early exposure to drugs, many of them were nonetheless adopted by single, black women—among them at least seven in my circle of professional friends.

The fact is, increasingly the research has shown that, given love, therapy, and lots of attention, a child exposed to drugs is no worse off than any other child born to poverty. To me, Charles wasn't a charity case; he was a gift. Though born to a crack-addicted mother who had tested positive for cocaine at the time of his delivery, he had been moved swiftly from the hospital into foster care. Since the age of two weeks, he had lived in the same loving foster home on Long Island, New York. As a result, postbirth, Charles had never been exposed to drugs. Indeed, he was so healthy and had such minor developmental delays that the foster agency handling his placement felt obliged to warn prospective parents that Charles's permanent placement might not come with the $500-to-$1,000-a-month subsidy that typically attends the adoption of a child from the foster care system. (While this is the only way many prospective parents can afford to adopt special needs foster children, the child's needs—not the parents' income—determine the size of the subsidy.)

I told the agency that I wanted Charles with or without

the subsidy. Yes, it would be difficult to raise a child alone, but after years of working in TV journalism I was financially set. Since my mid-twenties, I'd known that I wanted to be a mother someday. Perhaps seeing all the women in my family have babies, I never felt the urge to give birth myself. But I did not want to leave this world without parenting a child. I assumed I would become a mom either to the children of the man I married or to a child whom I adopted as a single mom once I was settled in my career. By the time I was in my forties and Mr. Right had yet to appear, I had covered so many stories about neglected and abused children that I felt it was time for me to step in and do my part by raising one of the children in the foster care system.

I had also been inspired by seven friends who had adopted children from difficult situations. As a married black couple, who had taken in four sibling boys all at once, put it, "If not us, then who?" And I could not forget one statistic I had read: One in three children in foster care is either a black or Latino male. So while thousands of Americans turn to China to adopt little girls who are not valued or wanted in their country, we have thousands of boys—similarly not valued or wanted—languishing in foster care right here at home. Though I had dreamed of adopting a little girl, dressing her in pretty clothes and teaching her to be a fierce feminist, now the reality of all those difficult-to-adopt boys struck me. If I was going to adopt, I wanted to make a difference; I wanted to show one little African-American boy that he indeed was valued and wanted.

By 1999, I was so determined to become a mother that I'd gone back to school for a graduate degree in journalism to prepare for a university teaching position that would offer more mommy-friendly hours. On September 18, 2001, the foster agency e-mailed me a photo of Charles. What a handsome smile he had! Two weeks later, he and I had our first supervised meeting at the agency. On November 10, Charles moved permanently into my Manhattan home, a rapid transition that, in hindsight, went remarkably smoothly—for the two of us.

For some members of my family, well, that was a different story.

On October 6, 2001, the day of Charles's first daylong home visit, it was so important to me that he meet my mother—his future grandma—that en route from Long Island we stopped at her apartment, less than a mile from my downtown place. She shook his hand—an odd thing to do, I thought, given that Charles was not yet three. For years, she had been a substitute teacher in various elementary schools. She, of all people, should understood what a frightened toddler I had on my hands.

As I watched this distant greeting that hinted at none of my mother's usual infectious warmth, I felt a quiet alarm go off in my head. Was she just reverting to the formal habits she'd learned during her British upbringing in Guyana, or did she, like my sister Dorothy, have major reservations about the adoption? Over the next few hours, my qualms evaporated as I saw her warm to Charles. By day's end, she had fed him, read to him, and nestled him lovingly on her lap for a photo (which, to this day, remains tacked above my computer for inspiration when I write). During that same visit, my sister Roslyn, who lives with my aging, frail mother, immediately hugged and embraced Charles. So did my eldest niece Rochelle, who back then also lived with my mom, and who now lives nearby and is herself raising a teenage son. I left encouraged and hopeful that my son-to-be would be embraced by our extended and extensive family.

But while my mother would soon come to refer to Charles as her "favorite grandchild"—which thrilled me—the rest of my family kept a polite distance. Admittedly, the timing wasn't ideal, what with Charles joining the family just as the hectic holiday season was getting under way. The crush of strange faces and personalities at family gatherings was overwhelming for him. Often he'd grow so teary and anxious that I'd have to scoop him up and leave abruptly. Still, it seemed to me that my family could be trying harder to make him feel at home.

At Thanksgiving, the oldest and youngest of my siblings, Mike and Lucie, respectively, offered Charles a sweet welcome, then proceeded to ignore him for the rest of the day. Over the years, I'd seen Lucie indulge and play with her other nephews and nieces; I knew she was capable of so much more. As for Mike, himself a father of five children, he was a seasoned dad whom I was counting on to play the role of patriarch in Charles's and my life together. Now I could only wonder if he would play any role at all.

A month later, at Christmas, Charles received a similarly cool reception from my oldest sister Anita. Though Anita is the most disengaged from the family of my siblings, coming home only once or twice a year, I expected more from her.

A veteran aunt, she had been Dorothy's go-to "auntie" back when Dorothy was raising the youngest of her brood of nine. And then there was this quirk: Charles, improbably, bears a strong resemblance to the Stainback family, especially to Anita. The first time I'd laid eyes on the e-mailed photo of him, I was struck by how much he looked like Anita at that age. I was counting on that resemblance to draw her to him. When she barely acknowledged him, I was crushed.

I knew I should be patient and give my family time to bond with my child, but seeing my siblings treat their newest nephew as if he were a stranger's child wounded me. Charles was the biggest, and greatest, event in my life; at the very least, I expected my siblings to show interest in my son. Instead, one by one, they each seemed to carve a path around Charles, exhibiting not the least bit of interest in who he was—which was not at all typical behavior. They had always been deeply interested in my career, firing off question after question about my job as a TV anchor. Now no one asked me a single question about Charles, an even more important part of my life.

What I read into their silence was a judgment that somehow an adoption wasn't as meaningful a life event as giving birth, and that my son was somehow less important than their children. I was furious. But I didn't confront them, because giving words to my pain frightened me. So did their possible response. Who wants to hear disparaging remarks about one's child? Thankfully, I was surrounded by supportive friends and colleagues, and was able to dismiss my siblings' coolness as "their loss."

In the coming months, though, everything slowly began to change. Time, love, kinship, perhaps Charles's unique charms, plus a few firm words from my mom, all worked their magic on my siblings. Charles, I could see, was gradually becoming part of the fold. When Roslyn's next quarterly newsletter arrived in January 2002, she formally welcomed him into the fold, treating his arrival as if it were a birth announcement. I was touched.

At about the same time, Dorothy, who pre-adoption had dubbed Charles "a stranger's child," arranged to meet her new nephew when she traveled north from her home in rural South Carolina for a family visit. By then, my mother had set her straight about adoption, explaining that while each of my fifteen nieces and nephews (and fifteen grand-nieces and nephews) were already in loving homes with parents committed to caring for them, Charles had enjoyed no such permanent home until I entered his life; it was up to all of us to help give that to him. Dorothy must have thought things over, because when she met Charles, she embraced him joyously and completely. Propping him on her lap, she unbraided and braided his cornrows—giving him all the attention she had showered on her other nieces and nephews.

Since then, "Auntie Dottie" has been there for me, offering steady encouragement and support. No matter what time of day or night I phone, she's ready to help me handle Charles's childhood illnesses and traumas. Recently, I asked her to be Charles's guardian should anything happen to me. She said I didn't even have to ask; of course she would.

Most of my other siblings have also grown closer to Charles. Mike now enjoys a fun, loving relationship with his nephew; these days when we set off for my mother's apartment, Charles hopes his Uncle Mike is there so they can roughhouse together. Though my sister Lucie, a newlywed, remains preoccupied with her new marriage, her husband Richard has thrown himself into the role of uncle with abandon the handful of times he's seen Charles. As for Anita, there are signs that even she is coming around. At a September 2004 gathering to honor my mother's ninetieth birthday, Charles played volleyball with various family members, using one of the celebratory balloons as a ball. It was his own personal icebreaker, and it worked (clever boy!). For the first time, he engaged Anita in a game. Later that day, she embraced and tickled him for the first time in their half dozen meetings. If their relationship still isn't as warm as I'd like it to be, I can see that the gradual growth suits the two of them just fine.

In retrospect, I realize I was perhaps a little too hard on my family. They had needed time to adjust, just as Charles had. As the months went by, Charles relaxed, and so did they. Though Charles still stuck to me like Velcro in most social settings, he began to feel more at ease with those family members who evolved into our day-to-day support network: my mother, my sister Roslyn (T-Roz, as Charles nicknamed her), my niece Rochelle, and her teenage son Garfield. Over time, my son learned to allow them to indulge him in the important business of child's play. Charles began to thrive, and my family began to appreciate his gentle temperament, his quick mind, his delicious hugs.

These days, photos of a beaming Charles enjoy a prominent position in the picture display my mother and Roslyn maintain at the family homestead. Now five, Charles counts on the support of the Stainback clan as much as I do. He loves that they turn up to applaud him at his soccer games and kindergarten plays. When I need a break or have a crisis (as when I was briefly hospitalized in July 2003), he has no qualms about being packed off to one of those four loving relatives on our support team. He relishes hearing over and over (and over and over again) how he has one (living) grandma, four aunties, one uncle, thirty first and second cousins. He particularly likes that last number, delighting in this evidence that there are compensations for being an only child.

In the upcoming edition of the family newsletter, I anticipate reading about Charles's first speaking role in his school's Christmas pageant. I no longer anguish about how my family may react to such bulletins. When those newsletters land in my family's mailboxes, I feel confident that Charles's good news will provide the same smile and dash of joy as any of the other young cousins' news. Charles, my promised child, is one of them now.

The Second Time Around

AMY RACKEAR

Somewhere along the coast of Maine, two Adirondack chairs sit atop a small rocky mound overlooking the water. Lush black-eyed Susans, lupine, and asters leave only a narrow path from the road. In the final days of August 1990, my husband and I settled there every morning to read about adoption. I surveyed the grounds and dared to imagine a summer when the tiny cottage we occupied would be too small. It could happen, maybe soon. After four harrowing years, Steven and I were finally at the threshold of parenthood.

My husband had wanted to adopt long before I accepted the losses of genetic continuity, pregnancy, and childbirth. Just days earlier, he'd rejoiced when we discarded our syringes and terminated medical treatment. Now, though we'd not yet done anything in pursuit of adoption, chance had united us with a couple whose unplanned pregnancy would make us parents.

Four months to the day of that first contact, our son was born. On the snowy evening he was placed in our arms, I believed his homecoming was a comma in our family-building effort. I'd always wanted two children, a boy and a girl, as in my own family of origin. Steven and I agreed about this well before our marriage. But as my interminable aching to become a mother gave way to parenting Ari, I decided to focus only on him. This, my first baby, was a star. He was healthy and exquisite and achieved every developmental milestone in advance of his peers. "Is Ari driving yet?" my brother, Andy, teased. A photographer wanted a poster-size portrait of Ari for his storefront. Our family of three was featured in a *New York Times Magazine* article that explored the shortcomings of advanced reproductive technology. By then I knew that the picture I had of my children during that period had undergone change but not compromise. Never could my body have produced such perfection.

Yet even as I reveled in this halcyon period, I remained certain that we would soon adopt again. I was, by now, forty, and Steven, forty-five. Meticulously, I saved Ari's toys, books, and unisex clothes, moving them, along with us, when we relocated from a two-bedroom urban apartment to a house some 50 miles away. Four of the new bedrooms were readily defined and gradually furnished as ours, Ari's, a study, and a guest room. The fifth, the corner bedroom next to Ari's nursery, remained empty.

Over the next few years, motherhood and volunteer activities more than fulfilled me. I went on extended leave from the profession Steven and I share, social work, channeling my skills and personal experience into helping others. I served as the New York City chapter president of a large national infertility organization. At the end of my term, I became its adoption coordinator. I planned to reenter the workforce, but I was waiting for Ari to begin school.

I was waiting, too, for a signal to begin our second adoption. Instead, complacency surrounded me. My husband and I knew no happiness greater than being Ari's parents, and for Steven that was enough. Time, and his own childhood, had altered his position. He had been raised as an only child for sixteen years prior to his brother's birth, and his sibling relationship largely consisted of babysitting before he left for college. Because of the age gap, two decades passed before they became friends. My own experience had been vastly different. Andy was four years my junior. I had loved him and played with him. I had resented him and fought with him. Always, I vigorously protected him. When age permitted, he reciprocated. Tattling was replaced by safeguarding each other's secrets. The friendship that emerged was like no other, and maturity enhanced it. My husband saw and understood this unique bond, intellectually. He could not, however, apply its significance to Ari.

I also lacked parental support. My mother and father had applauded our decision to withdraw from infertility treatment and pursue adoption. They welcomed Ari, their first grandchild, with unprecedented joy. Skeptical that Steven and I could be so very blessed twice, they thought that I, like my husband, should be content. Seven weeks after Ari was born, my brother and sister-in-law brought them another grandson. Three more boys would follow. Was it not sufficient, my parents argued, for Ari to have cousins?

A new obstacle emerged when Ari was a toddler. His pediatrician diagnosed a persistent cough as asthma. Again, I found myself frequenting doctors' offices, sometimes daily. Instead of infertility meetings, I attended support groups for parents of children with asthma. As Ari's condition escalated, vacations were frequently postponed. So was my quest for another baby.

I understood the dynamics that were stymieing me. If the seemingly perfect child inspires anxiety that the next one will be less, the child with problems consumes so much time and energy that parents inevitably question what will remain for a new sibling. Ari epitomized both. He exceeded all our expectations. At the same time, in those early years, his asthma often defined our life. Perhaps Steven was right; perhaps one child was enough. I tried to believe it and find closure.

Meanwhile, my energy was spent during asthmatic episodes. At night I listened to Ari's uninterrupted cough, rising in fear if it stopped, then rising again when the hour came to safely administer the medicinal steam that offered temporary relief. Rarely did illness curtail Ari's daytime activities. We went to playgrounds, library hour, music, gym, and swimming classes. Life was exhilarating and exhausting. Still, for me, it felt incomplete.

I remember exactly when the infertility sore reopened, and the sepia image I harbored of a son and daughter became black-and-white. I was at a weekly playgroup, chatting with the five other mothers as we kept an eye on our three-year-olds. We were acquaintances, not friends; given the nature of this particular constellation, adoption was never discussed, so the members were unaware that Ari was adopted. One mother had a newborn in tow. Another's unplanned pregnancy was suddenly discernible. The third was scheduled to deliver imminently. The fourth revealed that she had been trying for months to get pregnant, and the fifth, I deduced, was considering it. The one out of six who was quiet was the infertility statistic—me.

My eyes were riveted on the pink T-shirt covering this newest bulge among us. I sat on a chair scaled for toddlers, smiling persistently to efface any chance that my silence would betray me. I hated being different. Ari served me an empty cup filled with imaginary cocoa, and a cookie I could not see. When he tapped the infant's mobile to make her smile, something stirred within me. Not the beginning of life, like that under the pink T-shirt, but my body's stubborn stillness summoning me to find the little girl in my mind's eye.

"Amy," the very pregnant one began, admiring Ari's platinum-blond hair, azure eyes, and delightful disposition, "you sure know the recipe. Better get going, though, don't you think?"

As they all laughed knowingly, I drank my cocoa and ate my cookie. The longing I felt to complete my family had not been stilled by time. Again, I was wishing for a baby. A daughter. Ari's sibling. I felt once more, as I had during infertility treatment, that the world was very round, and I would never find my way to its center. Like these women whose bodies were stretched, I, too, wanted a baby.

Mine, though, I knew, would come with great difficulty or not at all. Yes, I wanted another child, but Steven did not.

This stalemate dominated my thoughts. Steven's resistance was increasingly impenetrable. Could I negotiate the process without him? Could I trust that, when he held our baby, love would conquer reluctance? If not, would he forever resent me and, excruciating to contemplate, her who called him Daddy?

From this impasse, miles of stress spread between us. Whenever Steven and I discussed it, my impassioned motivations paled beside his practical concerns. Our ages ranked high. Did we have the physical stamina to handle the demands of an infant and, in a decade, the adolescent she would be? Would I, in my fifties, be comfortable as the oldest mommy at the kindergarten picnic? A different kind of biological clock ticked loudly.

Our financial status, certainly, was another issue. Medical treatment, followed by adoption, had nearly depleted our savings. While I still planned to resume my career someday, for now a return to a social worker's salary was hard to justify when child care threatened to absorb 75 percent of my earnings. Even if our hearts were large enough to nurture another child, would this financial toll compromise Ari's opportunities?

I had faith that we would overcome these challenges. Yet I, too, worried, and Steven's arguments undermined my resolve to move forward. Instead, I waited for a sign.

It arrived some six months later. Ari was playing with his friend's twin dolls. "Will you buy them for me?" Ari asked, putting the pacifier into a plastic mouth programmed to stop crying when plugged. This I could give him, and quickly found the identical pair in a toy store. Later that week I heard from a friend, an adoptive mother pursuing another baby domestically. She had spoken at length with a pregnant woman considering placement. When an ultrasound revealed twins, my friend's husband refused to continue. Knowing I still hoped to adopt, she called to see if Steven and I might be interested.

Though not quite the miracle of how Ari joined us, when he seemingly fell from the skies, for me this sign contained enough magic to stifle Steven's pragmatism. Many who adopt strongly believe that the children who come home to us are meant to be ours, so I took fate's hand and convinced Steven it was time to proceed. Like Ari, I insisted, it seemed these twins were destined for us. He knew how much I wished for a larger family. With grave misgivings, he finally agreed to adopt again. I began a telephone relationship with the pregnant woman. Though potential medical issues gave me pause, I completed the paperwork. We retained an attorney and expedited our home study, and the court certified us as qualified adoptive parents.

Then the woman disappeared. Eventually I learned from my friend that the expectant mother had decided to parent her twins. When I called Steven at work to tell him, I was surprised by how calm I felt. Certainly, I had anticipated *his* relief, but I had not expected my own, despite my awareness throughout my contact with the woman that something did not feel right. Why had I been incapable of extricating myself from her and the twins? Was I scared that this might be my last chance? I had never before needed to be proactive and search for a baby. Perhaps I couldn't do it. Did I even want to? Steven, in his more magnanimous moments, might cooperate, but the decision was mine to make. Was I backsliding toward irresolution?

There was now a pervasive hole at the kitchen table and in the rear of our car. I saw my family as a triangle shackled by ambivalence. A new dimension opened one afternoon as Ari and I drove by the cemetery we so often passed en route to preschool. "What's that?" his bell-like voice demanded. How does one explain that your eyes close, breathing stops, and eternity is spent in a box underground? "It's a special kind of park," I replied, thinking I'd deftly dodged the question.

But Ari, though only four years old, outwitted me. That night, as the three of us ate dinner, he broached the topic of death with a determination that offered no loopholes. "When you're both gone," Ari said, "I'll be all alone."

Ari had not only discovered mortality, he also had glimpsed his future without parents. His sadness and fear were palpable. "We'll be here for a long time," I answered, "and when you grow up, if you want, you'll have a wife and children of your own. You won't be alone."

"Mommy," Ari then announced, "I want a brother or sister."

Rendered nearly speechless by Ari's loneliness, I managed to summon some reassurance. "Maybe you will have one someday." Then, I looked to Steven for help, but he said nothing.

In the coming months, I found myself often drawn to the corner room adjacent to Ari's bedroom, the one that fills with morning light. Despite the passage of years, it remained empty, except for the white wicker daybed on which I'd slept as a child. It was on this mattress that I'd kept vigil all through the winter night when we first brought our baby boy home. It seemed like yesterday. It seemed like a lifetime ago. Now uncertainty lured me back to my old bed in this unused space. I envisioned the walls covered in a palette of pastels, and a braided oval rug on which one baby, not twins, crawled. The baby was a girl, whose outfits I had been collecting since young adulthood. Could I still find her, and where?

Adoption is hard and has inherent risks. The domestic route that so easily joined us with Ari guarantees no time or dollar limit. Our experience with the twins, fortunately, was brief and incurred little expense. Nor had Ari suffered disappointment, because we had withheld all information from him. Through my volunteer work, I knew numerous people who had endured failed situations, some repeatedly. I was unwilling to expose Ari to that possibility. How could we prepare him for a sibling who might not be coming home? Losing the twins confirmed that a domestic adoption was no longer viable for us.

International adoption relies less on serendipity. At the outset, we would know the approximate time line and cost. We could even select our child's sex. This path presents different concerns, though. For us, limited medical and social information, and the potential effects of institutionalization, were the most salient. Relatives, friends, and some social work colleagues, biased by distorted media reports of unhealthy and unattached children, hastened to discourage us. Without wholehearted support, I continued to vacillate.

When Ari entered kindergarten, I launched a private social work practice specializing in adoption, and continued my volunteer work. That fall I coordinated a full-day conference for prospective adoptive parents. I designed the work-shops, engaged the lecturers, and attended every session on international adoption. One of the speakers was the direc-tor of an agency that had a Russia program. I'd called her for information in the aftermath of the twins; it was at this con-ference that we first met. Over lunch, I shared the details of my plight. She looked me in the eye, put her hand on mine, and said with quiet confidence, "Fill out the application, Amy. We'll find your baby."

That weekend I saw clearly the consequence of letting inertia make our decision: unless we adopted again, I would forever live with profound regret. I was forty-six years old, and opportunity was waning. I yearned for a daughter; I yearned for Ari's sister. My parents by now had four grandsons. This family needed a girl. I knew many people who had wonderful experiences adopting from Russia, and it was also largely my heritage. We would find our daughter there.

Just making a choice was immensely liberating and energizing. Again, I was the project coordinator. Again, Steven succumbed to my intensity. I watched his face the first time he saw the video of the baby destined to be our daughter. Nearly impassive, he was still on the periphery of our next great adventure, a compliant passenger. I sent the tape and the accompanying medical records to three pediatricians specializing in international adoption. Upon receiving positive input from each of them, we knew she was our girl.

After that, we showed Ari, then age seven, the video. No explanation preceded his viewing. "Is that her?" he asked, his eyes wide and glowing as he stared at the eight-month-old baby who beamed at him from our television screen. "Is that my sister?"

I looked at Steven. Ari's father was smiling.

On the night of our arrival in Moscow, the three of us boarded a second plane that took us toward Siberia in a violent blizzard. We met Tamar at an orphanage in Perm the next day. The caregiver handed her, wailing, to Steven. Instinctively, and instantly, he comforted her. The visit was short, and we were allowed to accompany our baby back to the room she shared with so many others. As we turned to leave, I saw Steven's and Tamar's eyes locked in an embrace. He was transfixed and, quite simply, in love.

During the court hearing the next day, Ari waited in the anteroom. Afterward, we joined him, and were putting on our coats when the judge appeared. She saw Ari and smiled warmly. Then she gave him a thumbs-up. He was radiant. No words were necessary or exchanged. Although it was not quite 4 P.M., dusk was falling when we arrived at the orphanage. We dressed Tamar in the snowsuit that had belonged to Ari. At last it was warming another little body.

My parents picked us up at the airport, and immediately dubbed Tamar, their granddaughter, the Princess from Perm. Just weeks later, Tamar's first word was "Uh-oh," and the second, "Ari." One day Ari asked me what time it was when Tamar was born. "We don't have that information," I answered. "But you know what time I was born," Ari objected, "and she's going to need that, too." I explained to Ari that I had no way to find out and could not lie. Then this intuitive, sensitive child proposed a solution that would protect our integrity and the sister he adores: "You can tell her she was born at night, since it's practically always dark in Russia."

Now seven, Tamar sleeps on the wicker bed in the room next door to Ari that fills with morning light. She remains very much Daddy's Girl. Every evening, Steven reads to her. By the time I follow, she is snuggly and sanguine. "I love you, Mama, and I'm so happy you're my mommy," she says. Undiminished gratitude underlies my own part of our bedtime ritual. I brush Tamar's hair, tell a story, and place a kiss beneath her pillow. "I love you, too. I'm so happy you're my daughter."

Color Her Becky

Grappling with Race

JILL SMOLOWE

"Mommy." Becky's hand pauses midair, Cheerios halfway to mouth, her features settling into the world-weary look ten-year-old girls get when confronted with fresh evidence of their mothers' ignorance. "Why in the world would I think about being Chinese? I don't sit there in class thinking, 'I'm Chinese, Miss Fern.' I just do my work."

She says this with utmost conviction, my fourth-grade daughter. Never mind that just moments earlier, we'd been pooling our memories to reconstruct a cluster of year-old encounters in the school hallway involving fifth-grade boys and some unpleasant racial taunts. She couldn't remember if there were four or five boys, if most were white or if half were black. All she could remember was that these older boys thought her Chinese looks were "stupid or funny," and that she told them, "That's your problem, not mine."

"Do you remember how you felt at that moment about being Chinese?" I ask.

That gets a shrug. "I just thought I was a normal person."

"Do you remember how you felt about the boys?"

"Yeah. I wanted to kill them." Pause. Giggle.

"Really?"

No giggle. "Yeah."

Bewildering stuff, this business of race. Make too much of it, and you risk grooming your child to forge an identity based on other people's insensitivity and ignorance. Make too little of it, and you risk failing to prepare your child for life in a country that every ten years maps its racial boundaries in such meticulous detail that the 2000 Census offered 63 different options. During the prelude to an international adoption, you sift through a (pardon the expression) Chinese menu of choices. By the time you've checked all the boxes and answered your social worker's barrage of questions—Will you raise your child to respect her heritage? Will you honor your child's place of birth? Will you instill racial pride in your child?—you feel that you've considered all the angles. But all those hypotheticals are a lot like the vows you take on your wedding day when you promise to love and honor your future mate: You really mean it—you just don't have a clue what it will look like or how it will play out.

In hindsight, I would say that my husband Joe and I gave less forethought to issues of race than many adoptive parents. Perhaps this is because we are secular in outlook, our lives revolving around each other, our work, our shared values. Uninterested in gatherings inclined to tell us how to think or behave, neither of us belongs to any religious congregation; political, civic, or self-help group; or association with a racial, ethnic, or gender agenda. Before we exchanged vows in 1985, we agonized over whether we wanted to marry, but we gave no time to our religious or regional differences. Eight years later, when we began to consider adoption, we anguished over whether we were too old to be parents; whether two writers could nurture the talents of a child who showed, say, strong math or art skills; whether we could give up the convenience of city life for a backyard and swing set. But we did not worry about whether we could love a child who was black, brown or . . . well, what color *do* you call Asian skin? In short, we entered parenthood with "race" relegated to the place it holds in our daily lives: far down on our mutual list of obsessions.

With a decade of parenting behind us, we continue to treat race largely as a nonissue in our household. On this particular day, it's part of the breakfast chatter only because I have raised it. Otherwise, as Becky might say, why would we think about it when other aspects of our identities loom so much larger? On a more typical morning, Becky ("student") and I ("teacher") run through her spelling words. Joe and I ("journalists") page through three newspapers, discussing news stories and hunting for items that will variously satisfy Becky's ("tween") appetites and our ("nurturing parents") need to stoke her interest in the world (yes, with a particular eye to China). We also tear out pictures of lions (a "race" that our *Lion King*–crazed daughter seems to identify with more keenly than Chinese people). The three of us go through these paces far more aware of the color of our day's attire than the color of our skin. Count on it: at some point my (literally) color-blind husband will ask, "Does this tie match my shirt?" Count on it: at no point will he ask, "Does my skin match the color of my daughter's?"

Yet every so often, issues of race catch Joe and me by surprise, reminding us that each day when Becky leaves the house, she wears not only her jeans and T-shirt but her skin. Skin that occasionally stirs notice because it's not one of the two predominant colors (black and white) in the adoption-friendly suburb that we carefully selected for its much-celebrated "diversity." Though there are Asian-Americans in the town, among them other children adopted from China, there are occasions when Becky stands out the way a lone woman does in a roomful of men. Becky claims not to notice when she is the only Asian face in a room. "That's just stupid," she says. And I believe she believes that—at least for now.

It is on those rare occasions when someone notices *for* her that Joe and I are left pondering what response will best prepare Becky for the world she will someday navigate without us to protect and guide her. Take her encounters with those fifth-grade boys. Beyond the thought of Becky surrounded by taunting older boys—a vision that would upset any parent—there was this unsettling fact: by the time Becky told us about these incidents, several weeks had already passed. Why had she waited? Whom did she intend to protect? The boys? Her parents? Herself?

Ordinarily, when something bothers Becky, she comes to me first. In this instance, she turned to Joe, the more easygoing of the two of us. To my mind, that conjured two possibilities: either Becky was concerned that I'd be upset and was trying to protect me at her own expense, or she was worried that I might make more of the incidents than she felt they deserved. (While she may have been banking on her father's greater inclination to joke than to probe or confront, Joe and I have a habit of mapping out a mutual strategy when either of us encounters a thorny parenting issue. We agreed that given Becky's usual tendency to confide in me, I would use a roundabout approach to try to learn more.)

Certainly, for me, the hallway encounters summoned memories of a two-year-old incident (to my knowledge, Becky's only prior brush with racial slurs), when an African-American boy in her first-grade class pulled back the edges of his eyes and taunted, "Cut the cheese, you're Chinese." In that instance, Becky also delayed telling us, then confided in Joe, again leaving me to coax the details out of her. When she insisted, "It wasn't a big deal," I responded (calmly, I thought), "You're right, it's *not* a big deal. But it is unacceptable. It's important that your classmate understand that he hurts people's feelings when he does that." A call to their teacher led to a meeting between Becky, the boy, and a guidance counselor. The boy was surprised to learn that his "slanty eyes" gesture was offensive and his chant hurtful. Becky and the boy hugged. Soon after, their teacher held a class discussion about diversity. Everyone walked away with a worthwhile lesson: the boy learned that words can wound; Becky learned that she can speak up and defend herself; their classmates gained a better appreciation of the world's complexity; and I discovered that the boy's actions had been fueled by ignorance, not a desire to inflict pain.

This time, though, several factors prompted me to proceed more cautiously. I was concerned that Becky might have turned to Joe because she felt I'd been too heavy-handed the last go-round. Also, I was uncertain how upset Becky was: while sufficiently disturbed to mention the taunting, she claimed not to remember either how many boys were involved or how many times it had happened. Finally, I felt that she'd handled the boys brilliantly when she told them, "That's your problem, not mine."

"I'm so proud of you," I told her. "I don't think I could have handled it as well."

After stressing that point several times, I said, "The school should know about this." I persuaded Becky to let me tell a teacher, but left the selection of which teacher up to her. I didn't explain that one of my aims was to provide Becky with an adult outside the family to talk to. She'd hesitated before telling Joe and me about the incidents; perhaps there was more she wanted to say.

As it happened, there wasn't. Though the teacher invited Becky to identify the boys, Becky chose not to (or couldn't). The school year ended. Becky never mentioned the incidents again.

Some parents, no doubt, would have pressed harder for a confrontation with the boys. But I was held back by more than the fact that the encounters were already several weeks old, leaving open the question, Would the boys remember what they'd done? My greater instinct was to refrain from a dramatic reaction that might deter Becky from coming to me should another incident arise. I also didn't want to magnify the incidents into something so big that Becky might wind up feeling self-conscious about her Asian-ness. Perhaps most of all, I didn't want to give a response that would imply that race should or must be central to Becky's sense of herself.

I remain comfortable with that response. As appalled as Joe and I were by the racial taunting, it would have been inconsistent of us, and therefore baffling to Becky, if we'd dwelled on the importance of her taking "pride" in her Chinese heritage instead of focusing (as we did) on the pride she should feel at having handled a difficult situation well, shaken it off, moved on. The way we are raising Becky, she is a multi-ethnic kid growing up in a multi-ethnic household. Joe's identity includes Cherokee, Episcopalian, and Midwestern strands. Mine includes Jewish and East Coast threads. Becky's Jamaican babysitter is black, Pentecostal, an immigrant. For years we've joked that Becky is the world's only Chinese-American-Cherokee-Jewish-Episcopalian-Reggae Princess. Becky's been to seders and Christmas Eve services, Chinese New Year's parties and Jamaican weddings. Annually, we celebrate a Family Anniversary to commemorate her adoption day. None of it, however, is the focus of our family life. For better or worse, Joe and I believe that to prepare Becky for the world (which we regard as our most important job as parents), we should expose her to all these influences. Both of us feel strongly that it is up to Becky—not us, not those boys, not anyone else—to decide which hyphens she will drop, which she will retain, which she will add.

I suspect my own feelings stem from my Jewish upbringing. As a child of parents whose generation survived the Holocaust, I grew up hearing "Stand up and be counted." Though it sounded important, I could never summon the feelings to match the command. Yes, I regarded myself as a Jew. But my connection to my Jewishness didn't come close to some of the other identifiers that gave me a sense of my evolving self: aspiring writer, loyal family member, hard-working student, attentive friend and girlfriend. I understood why my parents' generation of Jews felt a need to stand up. But why, I wondered, should I? No one was telling me to sit down.

The only time I ever felt an impulse to "stand up" was when I learned that the Christian mother of my high school boyfriend wasn't too thrilled about her son's dating a Jew. As soon as I caught wind of that, I made it a point to wear my long-ignored Jewish-star necklace every time I visited his house. I haven't worn it since.

In this era of global tensions and showy patriotism, I've come to realize that I feel much the same way about being American. I am American to the core. As such, I don't feel a need to advertise, flaunt, or parade it by hoisting flags or sporting pins in my lapel. My own impulse is to seek commonalities, not to accentuate differences.

Am I "proud" of being Jewish or American (or white or a woman, for that matter)? Apparently only if I sense someone would prefer I weren't. Otherwise, what do I have to feel proud of? For me, personal pride is a by-product of hard work. I did not have to earn my Jewish or American (or white or female) identities. They came with my birth.

So it is with Becky's Asian identity; it is her birthright. I acknowledge, embrace, and celebrate that, just as I celebrate *all* things Becky. But I am disinclined to try to dictate to Becky what her skin color, Asian features, and cultural heritage should mean to her. I'm not Asian; how could I possibly know? I also don't know how to instill racial pride in her, as the adoption literature often exhorts. Instead, I resonate to a comment made by a Native American adult whose adoptive parents are white: "I'm very grateful that my parents never tried to give me what they weren't able to give: my Indian self. I think that causes confusion. It was my journey to find out more."

To launch Becky on her own journey, Joe and I make efforts to expose her to aspects of the Chinese culture (though parents who send their children to Chinese-language classes and culture camp would find our efforts meager). Her bookshelves, which overflow with volumes about Hanukkah, Christmas, adoption, diversity, and feisty young girls, include books about China and Asian-Americans. We've been to culture days, Chinese circuses, the Chinatowns in various cities, a Chinese New Year's celebration at the Chinese Embassy in Washington.

I have little sense what impact any of this is having on Becky. As yet, she shows scant interest in anything Chinese, save rice. At three, a Chinese-born friend of hers walked up to a TV set, put her finger on the face of an Asian youngster, and said, "Me!" Becky has never done anything remotely like that. From the start, she proved as uninterested in her Asian-faced dolls as she was in her white-faced and black-faced dolls. (Stuffed lions are another matter.) She balked when we suggested Chinese lessons. She's indifferent to the various "Asian role models" we've put in her way: she dumped a Chinese piano teacher ("She's so boring") in favor of a Latina teacher ("She's cool"); she seems not to notice that her pediatrician has an Asian face; she feels no identification with her choir teacher. ("He's *Korean*, Mommy.") When we talk about a family trip to China that we are planng to make before Becky turns eleven, she harrumphs, "What's the point?" She'd rather return to Jamaica (home of her babysitter) or England (land of Harry Potter).

On this morning as I probe Becky about race, I ask if she ever thinks about being from China. "Never," she replies. "I'm too distracted with what I'm doing for the day." Does it bother her when people ask where she's from? "It's good they ask," she says, her tone practical. "That way they can learn what people look like." Her friends include a smattering of Asian-Americans, but that fact seems of little interest to her. "Meili was born in China. Big deal." Shrug. "Corrine was born in Korea." Shrug. "Eva's parents are from the Philippines." Shrug. About Eva, a close school friend with whom she sits almost daily at lunch, Becky adds, "People think we're sisters or cousins. We tell them, 'No, like for the thousandth time!'" Have she and Eva ever talked about race? "No." Did she ever tell Eva about those incidents last year with the fifth-grade boys? "Why would I do that?" Cue in the eye roll. "It was so long ago."

The question that lingers, of course, is what, if any, enduring impact that taunting has had. Does it make Becky feel less secure in the universe? Or stronger for having dealt with it effectively? Does it make her identify more closely with her Chinese roots? Or less? Does any anger or hurt remain? Or has she shrugged it off with the other bumps and scrapes of childhood? When questions like that start to buzz, Joe and I get to wondering if we are remiss not making more of Becky's Asian inheritance. After all, we've been told repeatedly, "You may not see her that way, but everyone else will."

I'm not as certain what other people see. Today's younger generations seem more embracing and less inclined to draw rigid distinctions. And older generations are hardly predictable. Not long ago, a black school administrator in our diverse-and-proud-of-it town made my jaw drop when he referred to Eva and Becky as "a pack of Orientals." I was no less astonished by a recent phone conversation with a dear friend, an African-American who's had a lifelong involvement in race relations. During our exchange, I referred to my family as "mixed-race." With genuine surprise in his voice, he asked, "Do you really think of your family as mixed-race?" From the tone of his question, I gathered that he sees only two hues: black and white.

At times, so does Becky. A few years back, she referred to a boy as being "not like us." When I asked what she meant, she said, "Well, he's, you know, black." I laid my hand next to hers and said, "You don't see us as being different?" No, she said. Hmm, I thought, was her response genuine or did it perhaps reflect a wish not to be "different" from Joe and me? Either way, time for some race education. "Many people *do* see us as different," I explained. "They see black, white,

Hispanic, Asian, Indian." Becky swatted that away: "I'm white, too."

These days, she would probably offer the same answer. Yet what *is* her perception? When the last Chinese New Year rolled around, an occasion we've honored in various ways (a trip to Chinatown, a party, an occasion to read favorite books), she reminded me that we needed to celebrate. When she shows her friends her adoption scrapbook, she points to pictures and says, "See, that's China." While she gets restless when Joe and I debate world events, she seems to listen more closely when we discuss China. Not long ago, she asked, "Why don't people in China have freedom?" and wanted to know when they were going to get some. (Then again, a paper she wrote about Gloria Estefan and her family's flight from Cuba precipitated the same questions.)

On this morning as I wind down our conversation about race—the one that elicited her impatient, "Why in the world would I think about being Chinese?"—I make a reference to Becky as Chinese-American. "No, I'm not," she corrects me. "I'm Chinese."

"No, sweetie," I counter gently. "You're an American citizen now, an American citizen of Chinese heritage. That makes you Chinese-American."

"I'm Chinese," she says firmly.

At present, I have no idea what she means by this. I doubt she does either. Whatever she decides down the road, I hope that I embrace and support it wholeheartedly and with grace. For now, I offer the best answer I can think of: "You're right, sweetheart. You are."

The First Thirteen

JANA WOLFF

I remember sitting on our newly and never before vacuumed couch—my husband and I answering questions as if it were the most natural thing in the world to be interviewed in our own living room by a social worker taking notes. We were on our best behavior during that preadoption home study—not because we had anything to hide but because we honestly could not answer our own toughest question (and possibly the social worker's, too): Would we love the child who became ours?

We knew a few things about love. We adored our nephew and our good friend's daughter; we got mushy around babies. But we weren't the kind of people who just love kids in general, and we couldn't assume, as biological parents do, that we'd love what we'd made. We knew we would provide loving care, though that's not the same thing as loving the child in your care. So we looked for clues about love inside our own wonderful marriage. Romance aside, love seemed to be all about "fit." That's when our toughest question got tougher: Would we fit with the child who became ours?

All adoptive parents go through the surreal exercise of "choosing"—newborn or older, healthy or special needs, same race or transracial, single or siblings—but fit is not a function of any of those. Even if we got the child we asked for—a healthy newborn of any race—suitability was no guarantee.

Fast-forward six months. My husband and I are sitting in our living room—on that same, never-since-vacuumed couch—for a family portrait: two blissed-out white parents head-to-head with a darling brown face of mostly eyes. Our biracial son Ari—African-American and Latino—was born healthy. The kid flat-out owned us with his perfection.

It is during this marshmallow stage that we and many other adoptive parents find religion—or at least reason to believe that there was nothing random about the match. It was clearly meant to be. That conclusion is reinforced by the nearly obscene joy of mutual infatuation. Sure, there is sleep deprivation and laundry, but the hardest parts of early parenting are outweighed by the headiest: you are your child's favorite toy.

Walls of our home document the highs and the highers of our full and giggly first five years. Even the adoption part—with the requisite grief and loss we'd read about—seemed instead to be a source of pride for Ari, sitting tall as his mommy and daddy taught his fellow kindergartners about forever families.

The questions we once couldn't answer became questions that got answered several times a day: Yes, we loved the child who became ours, and yes, ours was a good fit.

If the story had ended there, you might think this adoption thing was a slam-dunk, that the child gets through it relatively unscathed and that primal wounds don't leave scars. But the story doesn't end there. In fact, adoption seems to show up more in our kids just about the time we start talking about it less. No longer our parrots, our clones, our groupies, our kids mature into their true selves, unveiling constitutional differences that we didn't see earlier, like those glow-in-the-dark stars that show up only at night. Recognizing your child as unfamiliar, as I have, is a challenge—not to your love but to your ego.

It's a complicated, entangled, unfathomable mosaic. Honestly, the more I know about adoption, the less of a know-it-all I become. The experience is like that famous evolutionary ladder depicting a hairy primate on all fours who ends up as *Homo erectus*—only in reverse! As adoptive parents we start out standing tall, certain of the influence we will have . . . and end up bent over and humbled by uncertainty about how much of an impact we had.

My husband and I—earnest about our responsibility and goody-two-shoes by nature—went with Ari to culture camps and heritage festivals; we read good books and made good friends; we stayed in touch with Martie, our son's birth mother, and talked openly about "the issues." The payback, *we believed*, would be a closely knit family in sync with one another. But we may have been too preoccupied with nurture to give nature its airtime.

Thirteen years into the adoption experience, I can see that biology's impact is greater than my own. Ari was always extroverted, loud, risk-taking, and disorganized, but I credited those qualities to gender and age: In other words, I blamed them on his being a boy. The problem is not that Ari was or is any of those things but rather that I am none of them. When the magician called on then-three-year-old Ari (hand waving wildly) to be his assistant in front of 200 audience members, I had to stand on stage, too—proud of my darling showman and painfully self-conscious. He sought the spotlight; I ran for cover. When, at eight, Ari skipped off to find his bunkmates that first year of summer camp, he left me aching for another hug, which wouldn't come for another six whole days, when my husband and I picked him up. He was willing; I was wistful.

He yanged when I yinged, in big ways and small, providing daily reminders that my beloved son was a chip off someone else's block. When he put hot sauce on his eggs, when he hated English and loved math, when he ran for class treasurer, when he went on a roller coaster alone rather than not at all, when he preferred cold weather to warm, when he wouldn't fall asleep before eleven or eat breakfast before noon, when he could not hear that he was yelling, when he zipped through jigsaw puzzles with ease, when he sneezed his head off each spring, when he surpassed my shoe size at age eleven, when he drew beautiful battle scenes or race cars, when he carried a tune with perfect pitch or told a joke with perfect timing—when Ari was being most like himself, he was most unlike me.

And what was I expecting? I am an enlightened adoptive parent, after all; I was not looking for a mini-me. Paradoxically, adoptive parents like me are comfortable being genetically unrelated to our children, but we are thrilled when they resemble us—if not in looks then in likes.

In fourth grade, my son wrote and illustrated a 12-page story entitled "A Shark of Bones," and I thought I saw in him the makings of an author, the second in our family. His sixth-grade obsession with drawing race cars in perspective made me leap to a different but equally presumptuous and familial conclusion—that he might become an architect, like his dad.

Maybe that's why when Ari, once the proud poster child for adoption, told us recently, "Adoption sucks; you end up with the worst parents," I could see his point. Our fault is not that we're the oldest, strictest, dumbest, or most unhip parents in the universe (as he thinks), but rather that we, like many adoptive parents, persist in our fantasies about our children—shaping them if not in our image, then in our image of them.

High expectations of our sons and daughters are not the exclusive domain of biological parents. All of us tell our kids that they can grow up to be anything they want; and while what some of us may have in mind is president of the United States, many of our kids turn out to be only average.

There's nothing wrong with average, except that it doesn't give moms and dads the vindication that above-average does. If their children do well, biological parents can bask in the glow of superlative genes; adoptive parents can breathe a sigh of relief about the long-term damage that might have been done by adoption's losses; both are off the hook for their own parenting mistakes along the way.

There's another, more sinister interpretation given to the excessive investment of adoptive parents in the success of their children: The reason some of us scurry endlessly to enrich our sons and daughters is that we are nervous about our children's genetics and worried about a predisposition to choose one's lowest, not highest, potential. It's a disturbing notion in the way it recalls the bad-seed myth that assumes the worst about a child's genetic legacies.

I know where Ari's beautiful skin and ear for music come from—the same place his dyslexia originated. There's logic to some of our assumptions—ADHD, learning differences, and depression run in families—but biology also gets blamed for traits we want to dissociate from ourselves. Any parent of a child who is difficult knows this tendency. When our kids are oppositional or impulsive, aggressive or insecure, we look for influences outside of ourselves—and we don't look very far afield. We're quick to attribute native talents and good looks to our children's birth families but even quicker to ascribe aberrant behavior to them. Fragile mental health gets blamed on biological families; good mental health gets credited to adoptive families.

Recently, Ari was egged on by a "friend" to steal a baseball bat from school, which he did. Figuring out how much of his impulsivity is simply developmental, and how much can be pinned on his wiring, is yet another iteration of that proverbial question that is often asked and never answered: Is it adoption or something else?

You'd think open adoption, like the one we're a part of with Ari's birth mother and her family, would resolve the conundrum. Martie, Ari's birth mother, could serve as arbiter of what gets put into the adoption box and what does not. Adoption, however, creates its own dimension, shaping Ari as someone other than who he would have been—either growing up with Martie or growing up with us if we were his biological parents.

These days, Ari—like most teens—is generally more interested in peers than in parents of any type. And yet the relationship between my son and his birth mother is beginning to take its own shape. Where once I was the instigator behind every phone call, every Mother's Day card, every birthday gift, and every visit with Martie, I am stepping back as intermediary. Each of their visits, I've noticed, builds more memories and leaves more concrete connections.

A photo of Ari with his birth mother and half-siblings taken a few years ago sits prominently on his nightstand. During that visit, Martie took off a silver necklace she had been wearing for years and gave it to Ari, who has worn it since. On a more recent visit, Martie told Ari she's going to add his name to the names of her other children on a tattoo that she has on her shoulder. And the two have talked about spending some time together during the summer, even though they live 2,500 miles apart.

I still notice Martie's necklace on Ari, long after he's stopped feeling it as something new around his neck. It shines as a reminder, lest I ever try to dupe myself, that my son is a gift, not a given. All of us—birth and adoptive family members—seem to be engaged in a multiple-partner dance: moving gingerly, sometimes gracefully, to find our right places as the music changes.

In the process, we are becoming our own authorities, by default. Most of the adoption articles, books, and support groups stop at middle school, as if nobody knows what to do after that, which leaves parents like me and my husband looking for understanding close to home—really close. Our children become our teachers, which is not to say that we don't remain theirs.

The reality that my husband and I are playing a decreasing role in how Ari turns out does not negate the impact we've had as his parents. On his conscience we've sewn our best guesses about right and wrong. In his mind we've instilled a worldview made bigger by families like ours. Within his heart we've planted our versions of abiding love. The specific values and traditions we've passed on to Ari over the years have, we hope, taken hold, but the most obvious elements of our legacy are more superficial: family jokes, back rubs, magic tricks, code words, Dad's omelets, Gary Larson's *Far Side* cartoons.

The three of us are sitting on that same living room couch once again, only it and we are more than a decade older, and joining us are Martie and her two children, plus one of Ari's uncles, three of his cousins, and my mother. Okay, we're not all sitting: we're standing, leaning, crouching, and kneeling for this shot. I study that photo, now framed as a 5-×-7 on my desk, and smile at the unlikely collection that we are.

We are gathered for an event-filled weekend, along with 20 additional relatives and 150 friends, to celebrate Ari's bar mitzvah. Many of the people who make up his universe are there: school friends, camp friends, temple friends, community friends; relatives by birth, by adoption, by choice. We are the embodiment of open adoption—celebrating our connections to this terrific young man and to one another.

There was a moment during the ceremony that felt even more special than the many others: Martie and I stood on either side of Ari and took turns reading from a poem we adapted called "Legacy of an Adopted Child," author unknown:

> *Once there were two women who didn't yet know each other.*
> *One you'd grow inside of; the other you'd call Mother.*
>
> *Two different lives were intertwined and helped to shape your one.*
> *The first became your guiding star; the other became your sun.*
>
> *The first one gave you life, and the second taught you to live it.*
> *The first prepared you to receive love; the second was there to give it.*
>
> *One gave you a nationality; the other gave you a name.*
> *One gave you a talent; the other gave you an aim.*
>
> *One gave you emotions; the other calmed your fears.*
> *One saw your first sweet smile; the other dried your tears.*

One sought for you the kind of home that she could
    not provide.
The other hoped for a child, and her dreams were not
    denied.

And now you ask us what the sages
Haven't answered through the ages:

Nature or nurture—Which are you the product of?
It's both, dear son, and two different kinds of love.

Sandwiched between his first and final mothers, Ari looked out at an audience clearly touched by this new kind of bond. He appeared nonplussed as they wiped tears from their eyes and found room in their hearts for impossibilities.

When I look, months later, at the photos, I see something else. I see my long-held belief—that my child would feel whole in the presence of his parts—for the comforting fiction it is. Because unlike a jigsaw puzzle, where all the pieces lock into place and fit together neatly, adoption is messy and three-dimensional: populated not only with people and experiences you know but also with people and experiences you could have known. It's a contingent existence, in which who you are includes who you might have become. Impossibly, the pieces add up to something more than and something less than whole.

On a daily basis, none of this adoption *mishegoss* takes up much space. Topics like homework and cell phones, girlfriends and instant messaging, allowance and parenting—they all trump adoption most of the time. It's not that adoption gets less significant to Ari or to any of us in his circle, but it becomes less of something you figure out and more of something you figure in. As you and your children grow up, adoption becomes their thing, not yours. It's their story to tell (or not), and their relationship with birth family to navigate (or not).

I hope the next thirteen years will leave my son's self-assurance intact, although I suspect that there will be plenty of challenges to his bravado. Where once he was loved by parents powerful enough to make his world a safe and happy place, it's now just the love—not the omnipotence—that he can count on as he journeys forward. Before long, my husband and I will have to be as brave as Ari's birth parents once were: letting him go without letting go of him. It's a journey that, by nature and by nurture, never ends.

The Fallout from a
Less-Than-Perfect Beginning

BONNIE MILLER RUBIN

About sixteen years ago, in a shanty outside Santiago, Chile, I met my daughter for the first time. Despite the corrugated metal roof and the dirt floor, she looked every inch the Gerber baby waiting for me in a pink crocheted dress.

On the sixteen-hour trip home, she slept with her head nestled against my chest. I fell in love with the smell of that head, the intoxicating fragrance of baby powder and Isomil that had been missing from our lives for too long. For years, my husband and I had focused with a laserlike intensity on adding to our family, and this cherubic five-month-old fulfilled our dreams just fine. Besides, with a lively eight-year-old boy at home whom we had adopted domestically as an infant, and an abundance of energy, education, and resources, we felt uniquely qualified for whatever parent-hood dished out.

We were wrong.

Her toddlerhood was fairly unremarkable—perhaps a lag here, a missed developmental milestone there—nothing too outside the norm. But by the time she turned three, the first ominous clouds had started gathering. At her preschool, she adamantly refused to comply with naptime, wandering from cot to cot and annoying other children. Finally, after a few months, we were asked to leave and not ever come back. Even as I cleaned out her cubby, I chalked it up to an overly curious child and a wound-too-tight teacher.

Two years later at the kindergarten picnic, however, I could no longer deny the differences between my daughter and her peers. In the middle of a kickball game, upset at being tagged out, she grabbed the ball and locked herself in our car, bringing all activity to a halt. Through the window, I pleaded with her to rejoin the group. She leaned on the horn, while the disapproval of other mothers hung in the air like the aroma of burgers on the grill.

That began a decade-long odyssey into a maze of psychi-atrists, psychologists, and therapies of all kinds (speech, art, theater—even equestrian). Why couldn't she grasp the sim-ple ebb and flow of social interaction? What made her irri-tation threshold so low that the smallest frustration could ignite a blistering tantrum? When playmates came over, she would slam the door one minute, then shower them with toys the next. She would pull away from our hugs, yet scam-per onto the laps of strangers. Teachers told us they never had a child speak so disrespectfully—nor one who penned so many love notes, embellished with girlish hearts and flowers along the margins.

By second grade, her angry outbursts had her logging more time in the principal's office than in the classroom. The educators were overwhelmingly caring and committed, ready to try yet another behavior-modification plan, but she had no use for their charts and stickers. In the midst of a meltdown, she wasn't thinking about the latest Disney movie or an outing to Chuck E. Cheese's. She was unreachable, spurning all human contact.

The calls from school came with more frequency and urgency, until my husband, an architect, gave up his job with a downtown firm to work at home. With more flexibility and autonomy, he was the logical choice to be first responder. He could get to the classroom in five minutes flat. We'd lick this thing yet.

As time went on, though, it became clear that our problems could not be solved by mere logistics. Some subjects (such as reading) came easily, while others (basic arithmetic, for example) completely eluded her. She could not do simple subtraction even well into elementary school. But her academic problems paled in comparison with her volcanic temper, which seemed to erupt whenever she heard the word "no."

We consulted with some of the top experts in the country, who diagnosed her, at various times, with Attention Deficit Disorder (ADD), Pervasive Developmental Disorder (PDD), and Oppositional Defiant Disorder (ODD). Later, fetal alcohol syndrome and attachment disorder were added to the list. But it became clear that the doctors had no more idea what was wrong than we did. With no blood test or X-ray to pinpoint the cause of her troubles, the only D's we were certain of were our own: depressed and depleted.

With each setback, I found myself thinking more about her life before us. Was my daughter damaged by some toxic substance in utero? Or because she spent the first five months of life lying on her back staring up at the ceiling? Like biological mothers who beat themselves up over that glass of wine during the first trimester, I anguished over our choice of country and adoption agency. We had considered Korea, but adoptions dried up before the 1988 Olympics. So we turned to South America, specifically Chile, which had the lowest incidence of substance abuse and highest rate of education. We had waited eight long years for a healthy baby, and we had done everything within our power to stack the deck in our favor.

More and more, my thoughts have lingered on my son's beginnings and how we got in on the end of an era. In 1980, adoption didn't look much different from how it looked in 1960, when a healthy newborn, a reasonable waiting list, and a reputable agency could all be found close to home. It was all so reassuring and tidy.

Even so, during the worst of times with my daughter, I never blamed her birth mother. Sure, I thought about the mysterious DNA roulette wheel and how if it had stopped just one tick this way or that, the outcome might have been different. But mostly, I blamed myself for not being able to protect her. If only I pored over research longer, threw myself at this harder, surfed the Internet faster, I was certain we could crack this neurological conundrum. Tenacity always wins out over talent, I thought—and this time would be no different. "We'll find a way or we'll make a way," my husband and I told each other with steely resolve.

So we pressed on. We enrolled in activities like singing and ceramics, hoping to find what experts call an "oasis of competency," some strength to trump the deficits. But everything we tried just seemed to bring more failure. During a production of *The Sound of Music* her third-grade year, our daughter—in her nun habit—inexplicably lay down in the middle of the stage, while I hissed warnings from the wings. Sports fared no better. She would endlessly twirl in the outfield, oblivious as her teammates rolled their eyes and beseeched her to follow the rules. Soon she stopped participating altogether. The family camcorder stayed in its case, covered with a blanket of dust.

By now we had traveled to three universities in search of answers. The experts remained baffled as to why her brain would suddenly go on strike; they pronounced it one of the most complex cases they had ever seen. Of course, that didn't stop others—well-meaning relatives, acquaintances, passersby—from offering unsolicited advice. If I would just eliminate sugar, turn off the TV, practice "tough love," or morph into stay-at-home Mom, all her problems would magically evaporate. They saved their harshest disapproval for parents who "overmedicate" their kids with antidepressants—and our daughter had been on them all, from Adderall to Zoloft.

I wondered what some of these people would have suggested I do the day I picked her up from camp only to find her sobbing facedown on the sidewalk. Two hours later, when I was finally able to peel her fingers off the pavement, I gently eased her into the backseat and we made our first trip to a psychiatric hospital. She was eight years old.

By fifth grade, she was in a special public school program for children with emotional disorders. That entire year, I took a six-block detour to avoid our Dick-and-Jane elementary school—the reason we had moved into our neighborhood in the first place, back when we assumed our journey would be like everyone else's.

Still, we weren't the kind of people to wallow in self-pity. We held a ring with many keys, both pharmacological and environmental. It was only a matter of time, we thought, before we would hit upon the perfect combination of medication, therapy, and classroom that would unlock this mystery. My husband could move intricate plans from drafting table to reality; as a reporter, I had access to the best minds in the country. With every other life challenge—whether it was coping with illness, bootstrapping my way to a major metropolitan newspaper, or finding a baby—we simply rolled up our sleeves and willed ourselves to succeed. I was accustomed to happy endings; this time would be no different.

But with each turn of the calendar, our resolve chipped away. We were emotionally and financially drained and still bailing a sinking rowboat with a thimble. By the time our daughter reached junior high school, I had stopped thinking about curing, and concentrated on coping, using a perverse form of scorekeeping to help explain the unexplainable. Since both my husband and I had dodged cancer bullets, perhaps we had somehow been spared because we were needed to advocate for our child? Or was this somehow payback for a relatively angst-free childhood? Whatever the reason, I told myself, I couldn't ask "Why me?" about my daughter if I didn't also question the rock-solid parents, loving mate, beautiful son, and fulfilling career.

Not that life with my daughter was all bad. Indeed, her tenderness with babies, the elderly, and animals would make any mother proud. She was incapable of passing a homeless person without dropping some coins in a cup, and had a special affinity for cafeteria workers and school janitors—people other kids often treat as invisible. I cherish vacation photos—the one of her peeking out from an oversized rain-coat at Niagara Falls; gripping the wheel of a go-cart at the Wisconsin Dells; on the beach in Mexico, her arm draped easily around my neck—as proof that we had our share of happy family moments. But the periods of calm always dis-solved into a certain rage that made it increasingly difficult for her to navigate the world.

Incredibly, my husband and I managed to escape the marital problems that swamp so many couples with special needs kids. First, he was a true partner, on board for thera-pist appointments, teacher conferences, grocery shopping, haircuts, cleaning out backpacks, and just about everything else that had to do with our domesticity. We had a shared purpose, but different strengths—he was the master of bureaucratic red tape, I the seeker of new interventions—which fostered an appreciation for each other. And we both took great pains to be gentle with each other, because to do otherwise would have only compounded our heartache. Our son, too, emerged relatively unscathed. He was away at col-lege during his sister's teen years, the most volatile period, insulated by the same age gap that I had once fretted about long ago.

Despite my ferocity, I was engulfed in sadness. I longed to be a soccer mom, not a mental health advocate. By the time my daughter was in high school, I found myself pulling back from even good friends because it hurt too much to hear about this wonderful party that we weren't invited to—the one that included dances—the debate club, band, and, yes, even gift-wrap sales. Please, I'd think to myself, don't complain about how tough it is to get your kid up at 5 A.M. for swimming practice when I have a child who won't get out of bed at all because she is so mired in depression. Please don't subject me to the merits of AP Physics when I'm praying that my child will someday be able to make change from a five dollar bill. And please, oh please, spare me the outrage over your child's Ivy League rejection. It all looks glorious to me. I craved that life so desperately that I traveled to the other end of the earth to get it.

As my daughter turned fifteen, we had only one key left on the ring: An attorney specializing in education law, who could help get her into the proper therapeutic milieu, a residential treatment program. He told us, "So many of my clients are adopted, I don't even ask anymore." The comment jolted me—but also confirmed what I already suspected after years of noting a disproportionate number of adoptive parents at special camps and support groups, and in doctors' waiting rooms.

These days, our daughter is at a residential facility in Utah that has relentless structure. The skilled professionals are making inroads, but are careful not to overpromise. While we try not to look too far into the future, we hope that one day she will be able to learn a vocation and live independently. Meanwhile, we cobble together weekly phone conversations, care packages, and quarterly visits to resemble something that looks like parenthood. When I am with her, we go to her favorite restaurant and the movies, where she holds my hand through the entire film. She doesn't want to be in this place, but she understands why she is here.

Our home is quiet now. I feel relief that she is safe, but I am also humbled by life. We didn't cause her problems and, in the end, we couldn't fix them. Despite all our efforts, we were no match for a bunch of neurotransmitters. All these years I had thought that my achievements—the strong marriage, the good job, the healthy son—were because of hard work. Now I realize I was just lucky.

♥

THREE

Variations on Family

Which Ones Are *Yours*?

JACQUELYN MITCHARD

The young reporter is very nice.

I am nice, too.

We have had iced tea, discussed briefly the reasons that I wrote this novel of mine, and are about to talk a little bit about my family. I can feel myself becoming less nice, and it isn't because I am not proud of my family, my four sons and three daughters, my much-loved late husband, who died young, my much-loved husband now—the father by birth or adoption of all the kids except my grown stepdaughter. I take out pictures of my family—pointing out which one likes computers, which one has a beautiful singing voice, which one actually *read* one of my books . . .

But the nice young reporter has a more pressing question, and even before she asks it, I feel it coming, like a prickle of electricity along the back of my neck. She uses her pen as a pointer and trails her way along the clustered heads in our family photo. And she asks, "Which ones are yours?"

Now, the obvious answer to this is so obvious I can no longer make my lips form the answer: *All of them are mine*. I don't say it, because I know that this isn't the question she's asking. She wants to know to which of my children I've given birth, and which were adopted. Actually, whether or not I plead with her not to do this, she will end up writing, "Several of them *are* adopted . . ." And she may even note that while two are blond, a couple are beige.

So I try to play a game. "You guess," I urge her. But she doesn't feel like playing.

"I mean," she goes on urgently, "which ones are adopted?"

And then we have to stop having fun, because I have no patience for this question, and it transforms me from nice-lady-how-do-you-write-books-with-so-many-kids to Tiger-Lady-Crabby-Oversensitive-Diva. "I don't distinguish," I tell the reporter as gently as I can. "Neither do they."

And if she—or a dozen others—could read body language, she would at this point go back to the computers and the singing. But instead, she has sensed Reluctance, which attracts a reporter the way a seal attracts sharks (I can say this, because I'm a reporter, too), and so she burrows in: "You didn't give birth to all those kids," she says, probably having found the (wrong) information about the constituency of my family on some Internet site. "That's all I'm wondering about."

"Well," I say, "I don't distinguish."

"That's, really, and I don't mean this as an insult, it's sort of lying," the reporter ventures. "If you don't say which ones are adopted."

"Some were," I say.

"It's like letting people believe you gave birth to all of them."

"But it's none of their business," I say.

"Or like you're trying to pretend they're *not* adopted."

"Not really, because I said some."

"If you'd just tell me now. Let's start with Rob. Is he adopted?"

"I don't say."

The reporter purses her lips.

And so I rush to explain. I don't want her to be angry. I'm lucky she's interviewing me at all. She's only trying to be thorough, and I know she doesn't *mean it in a bad way,* as my husband tells me endlessly, when one of his relatives comments, for example, on how generous it is of Chris to love all those kids the way he loves his *own.* When a friend asks if I ever wanted "to give one of them back." Or if I ever thought that a teenager's acting out meant there was "insanity in the family." (I always have a rejoinder for that one: Not until he was adopted into my family.)

But I have to try to make her understand. And I do. "It's like my asking you, Are you married?" She nods. "And then my asking you, So, do you have sex with your husband?" She nods again, a little pleat of frustration forming on her brow. "And *then,* it's like my asking, Well, so how many times a week do you do it?"

"But that would be a really personal question!" she objects.

"And so is yours," I say. "To me. Because if my kids want to tell you they were adopted, that's up to them. But I don't own them, and I don't own their lives or their stories. It's like, It's a nice thing that you and your husband have a happy sex life. But it's also personal. And you can imagine how my children would feel if I took this picture and said, 'That one is mine, that one isn't . . .'"

But she can't imagine what her question feels like for me. No one can ever imagine. You'd think by now that adoption's so deep in our culture that the next thing we'll be giving our kids is Barbie's Chinese Baby, but our families are still a curiosity—still regarded as a little on the shady side of regular. We most often are not aware of it, and that's because we're used to being odd.

But how did we get so militant about it? Well, of course, it's my fault. I started breathing fire from my nostrils at the first whisper of such questions twenty-one years ago, when I adopted my first child. He was just a little sprout with a new baby brother when a kindly neighborhood teacher, on the soccer field, said, apropos of nothing, "Now, Dan's obviously yours, but Rob sticks out like a sore thumb!" (This woman's *husband* was adopted, but she went on to insist that her husband was "the only good one," as his siblings are "not quite there.") Three of my kids were standing there during this interchange—Rob, my elder stepdaughter, then only ten, who quickly learned to breathe fire on her brothers' behalf, and little "obviously mine" Dan. (Actually, he was asleep in his car seat). And while I was thinking she must have the cognitive skills of our pet ferret, and I wanted to shriek, *Are you nuts? How would you like it if I described your son that way?,* I knew that if I gave her a piece of my mind, I would be overreacting, because I should have known that she *didn't mean it that way.* However, when she asked, "Where did you get him?" she forced me.

I replied, "Where did you get your kids?"

She smiled. "Well, that's obvious; they all look exactly alike, three strong little boys."

"But how can you be sure they'll always be so, you know, great, since your husband is *you-know-what*?" I asked. "Have you done a background check? Do you know his birth parents? I know Rob's mother. She's beautiful and smart . . ." But the kindly teacher was already drifting away, and she later made a second career of bad-rapping me and my family.

Why? I had challenged her assumptions. She assumed that since I didn't have a "normal" family according to her calculus—that is to say, "biological"—she had a right to treat them as "chemical," as if they were interesting objects who might be examined under her personal microscope, as if they were not living, loved, sentient humans with ears to hear and hearts to harm.

It is not really adoption itself (which in our family is only one of the facts of life, along with no TV on the weekend and mandatory piano lessons) but what my stepdaughter once called DAT (Dumb Adoption Talk) that causes the many so-called "issues" that children who were adopted are supposed to have. I'm not saying that my children don't have plenty of issues. They're regular kids. At thirteen, my son Rob told me, "I don't hate you because I'm an adolescent who's trying to adjust to the fact that he was adopted. I hate you personally." All of which is to say, they've been schooled not with weapons but with information, to fend off this talk, with some rather pointed in-family talk. As in, "If you ever let anyone dis your brother or your sister because he was adopted, there will be consequences." (None of them has ever suffered "the consequences" but I'm sure they would be horrid.)

The subject comes up so often, however, even the kids are so bored that they think of novel ways to confront it.

"You don't look like your littlest sister," a pal tells my son Marty.

"Yeah, she's cuter," he says. "Must be genetic."

When I gave birth to Marty, my late husband, Dan, who died of cancer ten years ago, commented that he didn't look much like "his own boys"—to the consternation of the obstetrical nurses.

Even my "new" husband of six years' duration, who used to say that people *didn't mean it in a bad way,* has begun to act like one of us dragons. Just a few months back, when relatives at a family picnic asked him, in the presence of four of the kids, "Now, which one is . . . ," he clipped the conversation in the bud. Sure, he had an opportunity for "education." Sure, he could have said the obligatory thing. But it's too annoying. We don't know why it matters *so much,* and we're not naive. Our children are good students, and they don't get into trouble. While not Einsteins (well, one Einstein), they do nicely in school. The older ones had terrible problems with their father's death, although the first thing any psychologist—school or otherwise—brought up was adoption. The same goes for any school infraction or complication, however minor, from talking in class to a learning disability. "Adoption creates a deep-seated sense of anxiety and alienation," one school counselor told me gravely, shortly before he took early retirement and made his incessant habit of chewing on his pens a full-time job at a place where most of the patients chew on something full-time.

"It just creates another layer of questions," I tried to argue with him at the time. "And as a parent, you answer the questions. Most kids can look at Weird Uncle Harry and figure out that this is why they can curl their tongues, but not all mine can curl their tongues, and so I . . ." The learned counselor shook his head, gnawed his pen, and sighed.

Denial. That's what I'm about, or so people think. Dear little Mama-Wannabe. I yearn so badly for them to be *mine* that I think that they really are.

But I am not buying it.

And neither are most of my friends, many of whom have adopted foreign-born children, and who are similarly ready to engage when a slew comes their way, even in a congratulatory way, even in church. (An example: "Aren't you just the sweetest thing for giving that little black boy a home in such a nice community?" a nice elderly lady told Marie, patting little Eli on the head. Marie answered, with controlled vehemence, that both her family *and the community* were the lucky ones.)

Moreover, if my kids aren't mine, whose are they? Their birth parents'? Some militant antiadoption groups would like me to think so. They would like me to raise good-living young adults to fruition and then hand them off to the (good and decent but unwilling- or unable-to-parent) folks who handed them to me. I know my kids' birth parents. I love my kids' birth parents. If my kids ever want to see their birth parents, they can, but I want to go, too. I miss them, and our infrequent phone calls and letters aren't enough. Yet "other people" only see those shows on TV in which the valiant daughter searches for thirty years to find the father she never knew and falls weeping into his arms, reunited at last with "the person she really is."

Back to the young reporter. You know how often that scenario really takes place, I want to ask her? Often? If so, why would it be on TV? You know how often kids who were adopted want a real familial relationship with their birth parents? My research over the years indicates that's true in fewer than 10 percent of all cases, even if they want information, which, of course, they do, and which, of course, we provide. When Marty was little, he even brought to school pictures of Francie, her birth mom, and me in the delivery room, and told the story of how the doctor was detained at a Christmas party and I, a widow at the time, ended up, on the Feast of the Immaculate Conception, December 8, catching my little girl as she pushed out, while a choir of nurses sang in the hall about another single mom and the baby in the barn. ("But why wouldn't she want to see her *real* mother?" *well-meaning* acquaintances ask of my daughter. She does, I answer. Every day when I roll her out of bed before school.) Francie's birth mother is a gallant, darling girl, and a close pal, who keeps in touch. She trusted me, a single mom with four other kids, to be sane enough to raise this little girl, though my only family had doubts. Even she refers to me, in notes to Francie, as "your Mommy." I've sucked out enough bee stings and pulled enough teeth that we are certifiably flesh and blood.

Are my kids closer than is ordinary? I don't really know. It seems so. Probably because of my scorchy example, or because they are from a large family, they hang tight. They learned early to say "I *was* adopted" not "I *am* adopted." If pushed. One of my older sons, for example, on hearing the word "adoptee," was of the opinion that it sounded as though he'd had one of his limbs removed—symbolically what some authorities (they're hopeless) believe. He says instead, "Why don't people get that it's not a chronic condition? It's just how you got to your family." That's his comeback.

Two of my other sons closed ranks against the kid brother of a neighborhood bully, a preschooler who said he "didn't like the color" of their sister Francie's skin. Francie has beautiful skin. It's peaches and coffee-with-cream, and goes with her luxuriant hair that shines like a patent-leather shoe. If you could, you would look like Francie. And so, to the little bully, her brother Marty said, quite naturally, "I don't like your face either, not because of the color, but because you're ugly." The little kid ran for his brother, the bully. The bully offered to rearrange Marty's face. Marty's older brother, Dan, then unfolded himself from the car. He's six-three now. Later, Dan told me it wasn't really the little kid's fault, because little kids don't really see color; but their parents do. "They're probably Republicans," he sighed.

Yet even my closest friend in the neighborhood, when I related this outrage, admitted that her own blue-eyed teens were "worried" about Francie.

"Jackie, you're not like the rest of the world," she said. "And the rest of the world . . ."

"Is an ass," I reminded her.

We do live in a small town in a small state, and things might be more urbane for our tribe in Manhattan. But then, my children wouldn't be able to live on a farm and ride their Clydesdale (three at a time). I'm not willing to live in a place more nonchalant about adoption. I prefer to remain chalant, perhaps for reasons of simple perversity. If there's anything to that thing called fate, however, maybe we're plunked down here, in all our infinite variety, for a good reason. Maybe because we aren't like the rest of the world, we can help the world wise up.

As that controversial little girl of mine, Francie, likes to say, "We come from all different places, like America." She thought that up, little bit of a thing that she is, and made a speech about it to her second-grade class. In actual fact, she couldn't be more on the money. Though none of my children was adopted internationally, our Irish-Italian-Danish-American-Indian-Czech-Lebanese-Latina-German family is a microcosmic America. This is an adoption nation, in a way. If it weren't for adoption in the citizenship sense, there would be no United States as we know it.

And yet folks may get smart about sexual orientation, and privacy, and special education and disabilities and religion, but they never get smart about adoption, do they? Until they do, I guess I'll stay grouchy.

I really don't like to be a grinch. You can comment on the size of my rear end. You can even criticize my writing (although I'll cry). But keep your mouth off my family's origins.

That attitude doesn't make for my seeming overly polite or reasonable. One is not supposed to have a hissy fit. One is supposed to roll merrily along with comments such as the one that follows: A longtime friend tells me about her pal, whose husband suddenly died. Their adopted daughter—her words—is only eight.

"Wouldn't it be awful to be adopted *and* have your father die?" she asks me, knowing full well that my husband died, leaving four children, two of whom were adopted. "Well," she adds by way of repair, "I don't think of your kids as being adopted."

Uh . . . is that a compliment?

So I have to believe that even smart, loving, savvy people, people with driver's licenses and advanced degrees, do honestly believe that my children are a cut below anyone else's, by virtue of their adopt-tivity. And they also think that we, their parents, secretly recognize this but have such loving (and generous!) hearts we pretend we do not. Even when the actor Carroll O'Connor pleaded with the press, after his son died from a drug overdose, not to identify his son as "adopted," reporters insisted on implying a connection between the adoption and the drugs. Several years ago, I cut out a *New York Times* letter to the editor from a British scholar, who pointed out that many of the truly prolific serial killers (one) were adopted. No one challenged this contention as both untrue and scurrilous. Until that Little-Old-Mom-She-Doth-Protest-Too-Much me. (In a blistering newspaper column, I pointed out that most murderers, serial and otherwise, grew up in their biological homes.)

Obviously, the solution in our family, as a family, in self-defense, has been to neutralize adoption. Normalize adoption. Loosen the "adoption braid." Kick the spokes out of the "triangle." Marty, that boy born to his late father and me, also was adopted by his stepfather, and since he was just three when Dan died, took Chris's last name. "Are you adopted or is that your real father?" people ask him.

He answers, "Both."

Do they spar with one another over which are Mom's or Dad's favorites, by virtue of birth? Well, I honestly don't know. I don't know if, as adults, they will. I know that when my father died, and my brother, in a moment of what he now calls temporary insanity, said that my father's wedding band should go to "a Mitchard" (that is, his son) instead of the eldest grandson, my Rob, he found himself looking into an icy pool of eyes, various shades. In surrender, he raised both hands and quickly slipped the ring onto Rob's finger. "You didn't mean it," Rob comforted his uncle, who apologized through tears. Will they fight over our estate (if there's anything left), claiming genetic heritage, the way they fight over chores? I'd hate to think so. But so would a woman who'd given birth to all her seven children. Our will is clear: Share and share alike. We've always taught them that we are not their friends—we've deliberately fostered an attitude that the setup was the kids against the parental units. We have no reason to believe it will not be that way, always. Marty told his brother Dan the other day, "When I'm a dad, I'm going to name one of my kids after you. I'm going to name him Pees On Seat."

Okay, ours might not be a strategy for everyone. It's been hard work, all that emphasizing. It's been hard on the wits. Even the kids think I'm a little overboard mentally, but I tell them that's my artistic personality. I tell them that swallowing rage can give you acid reflux. If I don't get to quiz people who gave birth on the particulars of their children's homemade status ("Now, did you use a particular position to conceive because you wanted a boy?"), they don't have open season on mine—or yours. I've gotten a reputation for this style, and am considered publicly neurotic on this subject. So be it. Maybe there is insanity in the family after all.

The Day That Hallmark Forgot

JESSE GREEN

While his classmates cut symmetrical hearts from folded pink paper, one little boy sat sadly at the back of the room—or so I pictured him—with no one to give his heart to. That is, he had no mother, and this was a Mother's Day project.

He had a birth mother, of course, but he didn't know much about her. What he did know fully was his actual family: the two fathers who had adopted him nearly at birth. They were sensitive men, highly alert to slights that might compromise their son's (or perhaps their own) feelings of normalcy. That such feelings were already compromised by reality—they were, after all, the only such family in that school, and one of very few, even now, in the country—is a paradox but not a contradiction. They wanted their unusual family to be normal in their son's eyes, as any parents would. And so, seeing, or imagining, his alienation from the community of happy children in the matricentric classroom, they complained to the teacher. And pleaded with the principal. And wrote letters to the editor and articles for educational journals. Which is how they became, according to some New York tabloids, the Grinches Who Stole Mother's Day.

I know these guys: I introduced them, many years ago. They are not particularly radical. Their crusade against the pink-heart brigade might have sputtered out quickly had the responses they received along the way not proved (to them, at least) that their concerns were well founded. They were asked, Was there not some female in the family the boy could make his card for instead? (There was, but that was not the point.) They were asked, Why should the school remove from the curriculum something so traditional and innocuous? To the fathers it was neither: not innocuous by definition, because it "harmed" their son; not traditional, because even though the official observance dated back to 1914, it had long since been co-opted as a crass marketing campaign for florists and Hallmark. My friends countered, What was Mother's Day doing in the curriculum anyway? It had no educational relevance. And surely there were other kids, kids whose mothers had died or jumped ship or divorced and moved away, who were similarly estranged by the compulsory mom-olatry.

The trouble was that none of those other kids, or their families, ever complained. Nor did I, though I am also a gay father, when the subject came up at my boys' schools. While I was sympathetic to my friends' feeling of injury, I simply didn't feel injured; I think it's healthy for kids to experience and accommodate, in a safe way, the truth of their difference from the mainstream. In fact, I've been delighted when my boys over the years have brought home their handmade cards, given them to me or to my partner with their spent lunch bags, and said, "Happy Mother's Day, Dad." Or even "Happy Mother's Day, Mom."

The rituals and holidays and gift-giving orgies by which we signpost (and thus try to direct) our reality take on new and often awkward meanings when applied to the newfangled families many of us are forming. I have been invited to parties celebrating not just birthdays but adoption days. Parents of children born—even if not raised—in other cultures sometimes observe or adapt the festivities attached to those cultures: Chinese New Year, Kwanzaa, or for that matter Mother's Days (plural). Lacking the bright line of legal marriage, gay couples are especially open (or vulnerable) to these gerrymandered celebrations, forced to mark innumerable vague anniversaries instead of one vivid milestone. My partner and I don't even know how to compute the length of our relationship. Do we count from the day that Andy and I met? That was in April 1995. From our first date, that June? From the first time we slept together – which was not the same evening, mind you? Or should we institutionalize the date from which, having agreed to be faithful, we counted out the waiting period for any preexisting infection to show up on an HIV test? That was July 1, like a fiscal year—and about as romantic.

Because our two boys are now nine and eleven, it makes very little difference which of those anniversaries we choose;

none will be observed more than cursorily. We're too tired and busy. Instead we focus on the boys' birthdays, not just because everyone does but because their birthdays are the one thing they have always owned, and gave to us. We are religious about honoring those days with proper presents, as we are about no other commemoration. By "proper present," I keep telling Andy, who once gave me a remaindered novel in a grocery bag for my birthday, I mean a thing in a box. Not an "I love you," nice as that is, or a promise of a gift that will come sometime later, but a tangible item wrapped, knotted with ribbon, and delivered on the actual day one was born.

We give the boys what we aren't quite comfortable giving ourselves. How do you wholeheartedly celebrate the traditional milestones of family life when tradition utterly rejects you? It is probably willful that I can't even remember what day our status as domestic partners was made official at the Municipal Building in downtown Manhattan, though I know it was in the fall of 2001, because there were armed guards everywhere, and the pop of our champagne cork in the marble halls nearly caused an incident. Perhaps the event's lack of emotional resonance (though it was emotional at the time) is the result of our calculating rather than celebratory motivation in seeking recognition, however second-class, for our relationship: health insurance. (As the domestic partner of a municipal employee—Andy is a high school guidance counselor in Brooklyn—I am eligible to share his city-provided benefits.) Had we arrived with more romantic notions, they would have been shot down in any case. The line we had to wait in for registering as domestic partners was also the line for registering as lobbyists. ("I'd like to fake-marry my boyfriend here, and while I'm at it, urge the city to consider the myriad benefits of natural gas, the clean fuel!") Later, the suitable-for-framing certificates, printed on a computer along with our receipt, were slid through a crack by a bored clerk who had helpfully taped a warning on his grubby, bulletproof window: "Don't ask for a pen I don't have one." We signed with our own.

I had once been given a pen without asking. When I was a teenager, the local chapter of the Daughters of the American Revolution sponsored a citizenship prize, awarded to the highest scorers on a history test they administered. On Philadelphia's tony Main Line in the early 1970s, the DAR was still a going concern, even though the high WASP barons who'd built their famous estates there had long since given way to middle-class ethnics in modest ranch houses. Several of the interbred and overindulged descendants of the old guard remained, sitting stuporously in the back of my classes in junior high school. But I suspect they could not have passed a blood-alcohol test, let alone one that required some knowledge of the Constitution's Equal Protection Clause. So it was no surprise to me, though it must have been to the DAR, that the winners from my school turned out to be two Jewish boys and a black girl. That the award luncheon was held at the Merion Cricket Club—a vast red-brick pile infamous for its policy restricting the admission of Jews and blacks—was an irony not lost on our kindly hosts, one of whom, remembering at the last moment that the entrée was pork, whispered to me in a fluster,

"Do you mind being Jewish?" I think she meant to put a comma in there somewhere.

I didn't mind. In fact I was unreasonably delighted by the whole experience of infiltrating an exclusive club, especially when I was handed a prize for doing so. The rectangular white box tied with a blue ribbon turned out to contain a nice silver pen, which I proceeded to use, as much as possible, to write things that would surely have made the delicate ladies of the DAR faint.

Many years later, at the Municipal Building, signing our domestic partnership forms felt like another infiltration of mainstream life, albeit a compromised one. Gay people are accustomed to that compromise: accepting the imprimatur of normalcy when it is helpful and available, while making the rest up on our own. For me, it has always been a badge of honor that I needed no borrowed ceremony to prioritize and solemnize my human engagements; I can choose whom to love, and understand the responsibilities that choice entails, without governmental or religious approval.

But badges of honor are often really badges of injury, purple hearts for the disaffected. I remember the bruise of *Bowers v. Hardwick,* the notorious 1986 Supreme Court decision upholding state laws that criminalize private, consensual gay sex. A majority of the justices found the argument that such conduct falls within the nation's tradition of liberty to be "at best, facetious." Facetious? So be it. If the law could disregard me as a joke, I could return the favor. What was the law anyway but another exclusive club, the kind I declined to join because it declined to have me as a member?

So I stopped looking to the law to give me the recognition it gave other people, and began to disdain the celebrations concocted in honor of such recognitions, which now seemed merely snobby and frivolous. This freed up my social calendar, for the days we observe as a matter of tradition are with only one exception artificial inventions, not by-products of biology. Anniversaries are made possible by the civic fact of marriage. Bar mitzvahs, brises, christenings, and Sweet Sixteens sanctify entirely random moments in a child's life. Graduation, Mother's Day, Father's Day, Fourth of July: all are mere commercial or calendrical oddities, and I began to resent them. The only modern celebration that life itself insists upon is the day a child is born. And that was the day, once I had children—or rather once they had me—that finally began to matter.

Fatherhood, for all that it welcomes even the least qualified heterosexual, is for a gay man the most exclusive club of all. To have a child by any method, but especially by adoption—where, in effect, you steal the fruit of heterosexuality—is an extreme act of infiltration. And yet the responsibility for young lives is so neutering and normalizing that you soon identify more with what you've infiltrated than with what you've left. Seen by most people as a parent rather than as a homosexual, you almost forget that beyond the near circles of family, friends, and (if you're lucky, as we are) neighborhood, most schools, states, and social rituals still prefer to exclude you. All due respect to the Grinches, but Mother's Day is the least of it.

When I met Andy, he had already adopted one boy, whom he named Erez; before the first of our various potential anniversaries passed, he adopted another, whom we named Lucas. Each was just a few weeks old when he came home from an agency in the Southwest whose clientele of birth mothers was predominantly Hispanic. Because the agency operates in a state that is vigorously conservative (its sodomy laws remained in force until *Bowers* was overturned in 2003), Andy would have been the sole legal parent in each adoption regardless of my arrival on the scene. But by the time I had to teach my younger boy what name to call me, it was clear that I was becoming a father whether the law acknowledged it or not.

And the boys, no less and no more so than biological offspring, were becoming like their fathers. Not physically, thank God; we're happy not to pass along our pasty skin and skinny legs. If you know the boys' genetic background and look closely, you can see that they look rather different from us and each other: Lucas with his tawny skin and jet-black hair, Erez with his linebacker build. Otherwise you will see them as they really are: each other's brother, our sons, New York Jews. We needed no document to show we were a family; we felt like one. And yet each time a milestone was marked—each time I had to explain myself at a birthday venue, or adapt a preprinted form to reflect our reality— I felt illegitimate. (How many times can you cross out the word "mother" and write "father"?) It wasn't the way I was being treated by the people around me that made me feel this way; most people are kind. It was my own sense that the secret infiltration of an exclusive club—passing, in effect—

was an act of bad faith, no matter how lovely the gift you emerged with. Anyway, I had the gift; now the club had to be changed.

The process has not been speedy, though it was a Judge Turbow who eventually saw us in a Brooklyn court on a fine spring morning in 2003 for the "finalization" of my step-parent adoption of Erez and Lucas. We had begun the process almost two years earlier and sometimes it seemed as if the applications had gone permanently AWOL in the backlogged court system. But there we all were in our ties and jackets, waiting what seemed like one last interminable hour and a half in the dingy courthouse hallway, as other families got called in and then emerged, wet around the eyes. While Andy chatted them up and I stewed in my own nervousness, Erez studied his Yu-Gi-Oh! cards and Lucas drew characters from Captain Underpants, as if to prove how utterly normal they are.

When it was our turn, we were ushered into an unin-spiring law library and introduced to the judge. The boys re-acted in their characteristic ways. Erez manfully went up and shook his hand (much as I had kissed damp great-aunts in my childhood) and recited his full name and birth date as if he were at a spelling bee. Lucas, uncowed and uncow-able, told the robed judge that he looked like he was gradu-ating from college. (Turbow, who has a semi-combover, took this as a compliment.) A clerk presented me with the forms I had signed so long ago and asked that I confirm my signa-ture. Then the judge, flourishing his pen, signed too. He said it was "neat" that the law, at least in New York, now allowed the recognition of families that, not so long ago, were invisible as far as justice was concerned. He forgot to say, but was surely aware, that there was something still unfair about the process, even leaving aside the thousands of dollars in legal fees it took us to get there—fees that would have been unnecessary if Andy and I could be married.

Truth be told, I forgot that too, at least for a moment. Back outside, before heading off for school, Erez wished me a happy Father's Day, even though it was April. Lucas said, "We're officious now!" Of course, we always were.

Moving as the finalizations were, to honor that date as special would be to honor the day I finessed a bad situation and was altered by the law. I would rather honor the day the law is altered by me. For there is another wrinkle here: Although the adoptions are permanent and unimpeachable, the state in which the boys were born has declined to acknowledge (as they would automatically do in any heterosexual adoption) the new legal reality. Refusing to alter the boys' birth certificates to include my name, that state's Department of Health responded to the court order with a pleasant "Dear Customer" letter:

Health & Safety Code 192.008 states the supplementary birth certificate of an adopted child must be in the names of the adoptive parents, one of whom must be a female, named as the mother, and the other of whom must be a male, named as the father. It will be necessary for you to designate one father to be shown on the birth certificate.

Though we were told to expect this, it was no less shocking; we are exploring a class-action lawsuit against the state. If we win, or if someone else does eventually, that will seem like a day worth celebrating. In the meantime, are there to be no Father's Day celebrations, no things in boxes, for my family? Must those of us who are only grudgingly and incompletely included in tradition abjure it like Grinches?

Before I became a parent, my answer was a defensive yes. With only my own fate in my hands (or so I thought), it was easy to assume I would never want what was not willingly given. The failed world was rejectable, and with it its ridiculous ceremonies. When asked if I wanted to be married, I always answered that I wanted the Calphalon. That I cried at weddings anyway, and brises and christenings when I was forced to attend, might have been a clue that some sort of ambivalence was at play. Indeed, it was at my younger son's bris—performed, appropriately, by a female mohel who was herself a convert to Judaism—that I for the first time fully felt the power of even imperfect observances. Trembling not before God, but before my own life, and my child's life stretching deep into the future, I realized that in rejecting all rites I had given them as much power as if I had blindly accepted them. People whose lives are based entirely on dreams of other worlds never find them, if anyone does. The real work of the imagination is not to build false realities from false premises but to see what is true and somehow make it meaningful.

Adoption is, in part, an act of imagination—an act that biological birth requires, too, if less obviously. How is this new life connected to you? How do you make it yours? The legal fiction of finalization was useful to us here, in that it erased (or at least shut away in vaults) all other possibili-
ties. Some people see this as a kind of theft from the child—a theft of a "true" life that is somehow realer than the real one they're living—and see the choice not to ac-knowledge that as proof of the crime. But at least for kids adopted near birth, the "adoption wound" I am often told about seems to me to be a projection of our own concerns about legitimacy as parents. A healthy child, adopted or not, may be curious about the other lives he might have led, but it's a parent's regret about the lives actually chosen that is usually being expressed in talk of the wound. And yet, however fictional, it's a wound that becomes real when we pick at it.

Which is why I worry as much about compulsively hon-oring my sons' so-called birth culture as I do about strenu-ously protecting my children from the normative truths of their society. I would no sooner insist that my kids learn Spanish than refuse to let them read books about mom-and-dad families. It is not separateness and a sense of injury I want to nurture; children will be separate enough, and pos-sibly injured enough, in time, on their own. What needs nurturing is the imagination to see how the reality of who we are, and what the world is, can be reconciled. I was never happier with who I was as a father than on that Mother's Day when my older boy called me Mom. It was a joke and a truth and (because he knew how much I loved my own mother) a present, too. He had figured out how to express his unconventional truth in conventional terms. For him no less than for me, the satisfaction came in the complicated work of untying the knot that kept the thing—the gift of his love regardless of law—in its box.

Standing Out and
Standing Up in the Crowd

MARCELLE CLEMENTS

I can't say whether it's due to nature or nurture, or a combination of both, but I do know that my son, Luc, always has been a happy nonconformist. I remember when he was in kindergarten, he came home one day with the assignment so many adoptive parents and their kids dread: Put together a family tree. For a moment, I was nonplussed, but he was unfazed. I let him decide which images should be included, and soon we were cutting little ovals out of photos of Luc and me, his grandmother (my mother), his aunt and uncle in Paris (my sister and brother-in-law), a few good friends, and our cat, Minou. Conceptualizing his family tree created so little anxiety that what was most difficult about the experience was cutting the right-size ovals, so they'd fit into the little construction paper frames.

Two years ago, when Luc had grown into a sophisticated eight-year-old, his teacher asked him to decorate his writer's notebook with images that "express who you are." Luc's imagination could have taken him off in any number of directions, but instead he chose to interpret the assignment as a mandate to create a collage that included a bigger and better photo of Minou, as well as snippets of photos of the Golden Gate Bridge (a reference to his biological family), the Eiffel Tower (which may have symbolized either his adoptive family or his much-looked-forward-to summers in France with me), and one of his baseball heroes. This happy juxtaposition of seemingly incompatible elements seems to me to be an apt picture of my son's sensibility.

Luc was born in Texas, a part of the world where eclecticism is a tradition, the full scope of which I first glimpsed when he was six months old and we spent a week in San Antonio to finalize his adoption. While we were there, our social worker, Nikki Lopez, an unbelievably kind, tall, Tex-Mex blonde who often wore a leopard skin minidress and wildly pointy 1950s-style glasses—not your regular social worker type—introduced me to a teenage neighbor, an adoptee whose name I believe was Colleen. I liked Colleen very much, and it was interesting, too, talking to an adolescent who had been adopted and seemed to be quite peaceful about it. I was curious about her history, though I worried it might be a sensitive topic. Finally, one afternoon, phrasing my question as tactfully as I could, I asked whether she knew her ethnic background. She laughed.

"My background is Heinz 57," she said.

"Heinz 57?" I repeated, to indicate my perfect lack of understanding. I didn't even understand that she was referring to ketchup. Although I have lived in the United States since I was ten years old, I had never seen a reason to adulterate a hamburger or French fries with a condiment (though I must admit that Luc's enthusiastic example has since led me to discover otherwise). But Colleen and Nikki explained that the Heinz people once boasted of 57 varieties in their product line and that, used metaphorically, the term was therefore a logical designation for someone whose ethnic heritage was extremely rich and complex. Or as Colleen put it with what was clearly habitual good humor, "I can't even begin to keep track."

I loved this term. Luc was certainly a Heinz 57 baby: His birth parents' ancestors had been English, Czech, French, German, Jewish, Choctaw, and Cherokee—for starters. And in a way, I felt kind of Heinz 57 myself. Or at least Heinz 7 or so, because my parents were French Jews who were both born in Poland; then, of course, once we moved to New York, who knew what we all were. Socioculturally, I felt I could claim a nice bouquet of flavors, especially now that I had substantially augmented my collection of demographic categories by becoming an older single mother who had adopted a child in Texas.

It often seems to me when I am with friends whose children are from Texas, Romania, Bulgaria, China, and heaven knows where else, that there is something enchanting about all these little bundles of mystery in our midst. And I know all too well about the dangerous cultural contradictions, the threat of incurable alienation, the unknown effects of past neglect, early deprivation, orphanage abuse, all the potential disasters that are constantly thrust into our consciousness by press reports, usually unqualified by any reminders that the great majority of adoptions result in good families—some of the very best families, only different.

Different, difference, distance from the norm—these are notions laden with contradictions in the context of adoption. Certainly, a profound spurning of difference is the basis of the invention of the dreaded "adopted child syndrome," a concept created by psychologist David Kirschner and first used as a defense in the 1984 trial of an adolescent adoptee accused of setting fire to his home and murdering his parents. Kirschner believed that an adopted child is unable to reconcile the part of himself that belonged to his birth family with the part of himself that belongs to his new, adoptive family; as a result, he remains forever painfully split, psychologically incomplete, and doomed to develop an antisocial personality. The "adopted child syndrome" has been cited as scientific evidence that adopted adolescents are at high risk of becoming liars, thieves, and serial killers, or at the very least, will be so lacking in a sense of identity that their psychotherapy bills will drain their parents' bank accounts. Never mind that Kirschner's supposed findings were quickly refuted by respected studies, and that Kirschner himself eventually renounced his theory.

Still, some version of this thinking persists in our culture. There is this notion, for instance, that wandering out of one's genetic backyard inevitably leads to flawed parenting, because adoptive parents unconsciously reject the adopted child, who reminds them of their own inability to conceive; the child then supposedly attempts to remedy that rejection—along with the initial maternal rejection—through a tormenting quest to find his biological family.

As a result, adoptive parents have had little choice but to assert that their children—and their own parenting—are indeed "normal." That's understandable. And yet, I feel that something is lost by not acknowledging the fact that, on the contrary, we who became parents by different means are pleased and proud of our different families. Many of us, in fact, delight in our children's difference. We find that scary leap toward the unknown future that we will shape together to be not only the most rewarding risk we have ever taken but also the most romantic adventure. Even the mystery of a baby's genetic background—the great media bugaboo—is, to at least some of us, a source of wonder and pleasure.

I have often repeated to Luc what I had learned from his birth parents about his biological forebears, and both of us have remained very proud of his Heinz 57 ethnicity, the ancestors who fought on both sides at the Alamo, the Jewish great-grandmother who married the Native American who worked on the Golden Gate Bridge. In fact, if anything, I have added to Luc's cosmopolitan ways by speaking French with him from Day One, and taking him to France, where I was born, as often as I could. As soon as he could talk, his French became nearly indistinguishable from that of natives—especially when he proudly repeated the dirty words he learned from the other boys in day camp. He adapted easily to being a bilingual, bicultural child. He loves going to Paris and eating pâté, mussels served with French fries on the side (no ketchup), oysters on the half shell, and filets mignons cooked only until blue, and even finishing a meal with rather smelly cheese. And because my family is Jewish, he is also a fan of matzo ball soup (French-style) and actually likes gefilte fish—with plenty of horseradish. Like any normal French person, he enjoys wearing fancy clothes and reading book-length comic books and willingly spends hours at the table, conversing.

But what was pure Luc was that back in New York each fall, he didn't relinquish his love of French cuisine just because he returned to his beloved hamburgers with ketchup. Instead, he amalgamated his preferences. Even as a toddler, he pleaded to have French books read to him before going to sleep, this at the same time he was an ardent (and extremely disorderly) collector of Yu-Gi-Oh! cards. But then his Franco-American duality somehow morphed into a predilection for cultural diversity. For example, he loved hanging out with the playful and mischievous boys who resemble him, but in a distinct break with the most hallowed conventions of his peer group, he also found the company of girls to be fun. ("Fun" has always been his highest compliment.)

Perhaps as a result, even while he was already drawn to baseball with the profound, powerful instinct of any true-blue American boy, when our neighbor's daughter signed up for a modern dance class at the local Y, he—then age three and a half or so—went along, albeit cautiously at first. When he saw that modern dance called for running and leaping about in a big bare room, and then sitting or lying on the floor with a really fun teacher, pretending to be various animals, he was delighted to join the class, and then to reenlist for term after term. He had a realistic acceptance of the un-likelihood that another member of his gender would join the class, but it turned out he actually enjoyed being the only boy. He took full advantage not only of his masculine energy to run faster than the girls and leap higher, but also to be helpful and chivalrous (more or less) because Debbie, the rather wacky and very wise teacher, designated Luc as her assistant, and he got to help carry the props back and forth. Like the girls, he remained in the class for about four years, even when it evolved into preballet, despite his male friends' bald reactions of revulsion.

Alas, they wore him down at last, and around the time he entered second grade his decision to defect was sealed by the fact that Debbie had moved on and had been re-placed by an infinitely less fun teacher, who focused on the more restrictive discipline of the barre, and never ordered the young dancers to run and leap about and then pretend they were animals. But he always remained loyal to Debbie and to dance, declaring to whoever would hear it that it was an excellent preparation for, say, basketball.

There are many instances I could cite, before and after Luc's brief but glorious stint as a modern dancer, of his ca-pacity for unconventional choices, and nearly all were happy experiences. But there's also a price, of course, for not con-forming. The problems materialized as soon as Luc started kindergarten and his friends reached the stage of asking questions he wasn't able to answer to their satisfaction. He may have been proud and happy of his self-made family tree, but it was bewildering to his classmates, and their ques-tions proliferated. What does "adopted" mean? Where are your *real* parents? Why isn't your mom married? Suddenly, he was forced to explain the why and how of the many ways in which he was different from them—in effect to account for his very existence. It was hard for him, even though we had talked of these things many times and, like me, he had learned to use the words adoption, adopted, adoptive, and biological—even if he did pronounce it "biogilogical." We had looked together at photos of his birth family. We had read special books that celebrated adoption. I made sure we saw friends who also had unusual families, and fortunately for all involved, there is no dearth of adoptive parents—even those who are older single mothers—at least in places like New York City. I had thought we were set, and I wasn't at all prepared for the kindergarten onslaught.

The most difficult phase came when one of his oldest friends turned on him with the scary intensity that can only emanate from a boy whose peace of mind had recently been ruined by his mom's giving birth to yet another baby—as if the arrival of one little brother hadn't been tragic enough. When he came over after school, he'd ostentatiously look around. "Where's your dad, Luc?" he would ask, every single time, despite both Luc's and then my own reminder that there was no dad. "Is he dead? How come he's never here?" I remember how one afternoon on a bus on the way home, he loudly lectured Brother #2 about why a younger brother had to listen to an older brother, that this is how things work in families. And then he added, turning to Luc, "Oh, but this is only for us because we *have* a family." Even the little brother looked away sheepishly. Luc pretended not to have heard. When I tried to respond to his friend's remark, all three boys gazed into the middle distance. What's worse, once we were home and, an hour later, I brought up the incident on the bus, Luc assured me he had no recollection of it.

When I saw that my own explanations would not suffice, I called the mother of Luc's friend, and the cutting remarks ended, so far as I knew. Unfortunately, it was too late to dispel the dark cloud that had drifted toward Luc's horizon, especially when combined with the blow to self-esteem that a large public school kindergarten and a beleaguered teacher can deliver to a little boy. Luckily (or rather, characteristically), Luc hung in there, willing to talk things through as best he could. At least at home. I'm not sure what he did in school. I'll never forget the look he had on that bus when he pretended not to have heard his friend's remark.

But it was clear, too, that aside from the psychological pressures of being an adopted child of a single mother, there was also an aspect of all this that was like a heightened version of what every child copes with when his sense of normalcy is threatened. Who can say whether one child suffers more from the insensitive taunting about his origins by his classmates than his friend who must endure the catastrophic intrusion of a brand-new sibling into what had once seemed like a perfect setup?

The crisis subsided at last, the way a violent tide recedes, leaving us to repair the damage and to try to be more ready for the inevitable recurrence. Luc reverted to his own nature, and soon was back on the lookout for new and better fun—whether or not it corresponded to his peer group's criteria of what was conceivable fun. Last year, when he was in the fourth grade, he joined a wonderful chorus, which would be unexceptional, since he loves music, if it weren't for the fact that this chorus has always been composed entirely of children of color. We didn't know this the morning when, somewhat bedraggled and disoriented by the early hour, we showed up at auditions for the Kidz-to-Kidz chorus at the big public school that also houses Luc's small progressive program. We were invited into the music room by a very imposing, very handsome woman wearing a long flowing garment and a matching headdress, and only then saw the tidy rows of children—some thirty of them—all gazing at Luc with flagrant curiosity. We sat down at the back of the room, and when, a moment later, Ms. Sandra Boozebailey hit that first rich chord on the electric piano and the children began to sing, both of us were goners. It was an extraordinary experience.

Six months later, Luc was on stage, singing and dancing with his new friends. The Kidz-to-Kidz chorus even put on a show for Luc's school. Despite his admitted fear that his friends would view his performance in the same spirit of horror with which they had once responded to his modern dance career, on the contrary and to his immense relief and gratification—and mine—he was the toast of the fourth grade, and the class bully actually declared himself to be Luc's bodyguard for the day.

How did Luc become so open to unusual pursuits and so easily adaptable to various subcultures? I can make some guesses, but ultimately it's as difficult to account for this quality as it is to explain the wordless, thrilling, transcending force in human nature that adoptive parents and children tap into when they form a bond that mimics or replaces the generational links of DNA, and feels just as indissoluble. I sometimes think about this when I look at my son (insofar as one has any time to think when in the company of a ten-year-old), because it is so interesting to dream about what preceded our life together and what may follow, how everything that makes him uniquely Luc may someday produce an unusually charming and tolerant man who is a gastronomic sophisticate, a great musician, perhaps a globe-trotting architect—or even, if his dearest wish is realized, merely a baseball star.

Divorce, Adoption-Style

ANTOINETTE MARTIN

This is not going to happen. How could this happen after what it took for us to become a family? Ted announced the day after Christmas that he wants a divorce. He's been distant and I've been angry for much too long a time. But this? He thinks we can just take apart the family? We got through seven years of infertility treatment together. We lost a baby together—a tiny perfect little girl, stillborn. That could have finished us. But we soldiered on, down a new path with pots of gold at the end. He can't leave our kids! Their birth moms chose us to be parents forever. He won't do this. No. It is not going to happen. —December 1997

I'm not leaving them! I'm leaving you."

I remember Ted, who is on the whole mild-mannered but with a tongue like an adder when provoked, uttering those words in front of our therapist.

"That's impossible. We're a family," I kept repeating as, in my daze, I tried to find the carpet with my feet. "We're both the parents of our kids."

He shook his head in frustration. "I've made my decision. I'm doing it."

Mia and Charlie were only five and seven when Ted, in the fourteenth year of our marriage, abruptly announced that he wanted to go—and shortly thereafter told me that he was already in love with someone else. Within a week, he was apartment hunting. "The kids are too young," I insisted. "They can't take this all at once."

"No," Ted countered. "It's *you* who can't take it."

He was right about that. I'm a slow processor, and that was one huge load of gravel to digest. But I did fear in my gut that the kids might have it even worse. While Ted spoke about the relative resiliency of children, I imagined cataclysm if our two precious babes even heard the word "divorce."

They are open-adoption kids, aware from the dawn of their understanding that their birth parents were unable to give them stable families. When each became old enough to ask for details, we—along with their birth moms, with whom we keep in touch—buffered hard facts with reassurances that *this* family was solid and lasting. Now Dad had changed his mind about Mom. How could Charlie and Mia possibly believe that they were still safe, still unconditionally loved?

When I couldn't convince Ted to reconsider the marriage, I begged him to reconsider moving out right away. When the marriage counselor added his view that we should take some time to decide how best to help the kids handle the shock, Ted offered to wait a few weeks—and forfeit the deposit on the first place he'd found. But I knew that wasn't going to be nearly enough breathing room for me. I was stuck in my Armageddon nightmares of the ground opening beneath my children's feet, huge ax blades swooping down on their little bodies, giant oak trees crashing over their beds as they slept. If I was going to mother them through this, I first had to overcome the dread monsters that haunted me, before the kids caught wind such apparitions existed. I simply didn't know how long that would take. Meanwhile, Ted remained hell-bent on starting his new life.

One early spring day, as the four of us were hiking in the woods and the kids had run up ahead, I made this proposal: Maybe he could leave me, but continue to live with us for the indefinite future. Maybe he could try out the new relationship—but keep Mia and Charlie in the dark about it for now, while I tried to get things in order for us three to start over, too. I'd try to get my head straight, then I would try to prepare the kids to understand a few basics about divorce without saying specifically that's where we were headed. Then I would search for a new, less expensive house.

He went for it.

The next six months were excruciating, both for me—because I wound up feeling martyred—and for Ted, who felt restrained and increasingly torn apart. It wasn't great for the kids either. Suddenly, Daddy was always taking "private time," as we called it, to go to Manhattan to attend a concert or the ballet or to dine at a new sushi restaurant. He was at an adult birthday party (with his beeper off) the night Charlie's beloved lizard died. Mia was mad that Dad wasn't there a lot of nights to read and sing her to sleep. "I don't like Dad's privacy," she complained to me. "Why does he have to have this privacy?"

Despite her distress, even I could not worry inordinately about Mia. She had emerged from Angie's womb with the kind of big-gulps joy and unsinkable optimism that my own anxiety-ridden blood relations can only gaze upon with awe. I knew in my bones that her emotions would be hammered hard by what was to come. But in clear moments, I also knew that this particular child did in fact possess the resilience Ted liked to ascribe to kids in general.

But Charlie? I worried every minute of the day about our smart, sensitive first child, who by second grade had already agonized plenty about his life having been changed without his consent, or even his consciousness, when he was nine months old. "I know people don't just trade kids like base-ball players," he once said to me of his adoption. "But I just want to know: When I'm older, like twelve or thirteen, could I go back to live with Angel and my brothers if I wanted to?"

At seven, he seemed precociously wary, often holding himself apart, refusing to slide into attachments that could be broken or lost. He was a natural athlete but never seemed comfortable as part of a team. He would glower, on the edge of tears, if he failed to skate fast enough, or hit the ball hard enough, or maneuver past the goalie enough times to prove indisputably to fans, his teammates—himself—that he was the most valuable and least expendable player anyone had ever seen. Our son mostly employed his superb verbal skills to concoct skyscraper-tall tales of his own omnipotence, rather than to explain what was in his heart.

What can I say? When I looked at him, I saw vulnerability oozing from every pore, and wanted to throw myself in the way of any slight or harm that might cross his path. (I still feel that way, though it's pretty silly to think of wimpy old Mom being the white knight for a fourteen-year-old with biceps of steel.)

After six months' time, Ted had finally had enough of my waiting and worrying. One night while the kids slept, he moved some things to his new apartment. The next day we all went out for Chinese food, and Ted and I broke the news. Charlie collapsed in my lap as if he'd been shot. He closed his eyes and did not make a sound. Mia bolted out of her chair and threw herself into Ted's arms, shouting, "No! No! No!" We hugged them a long time. We said, "Of course, you will be part of Dad's new life, too." Then Ted asked if they wanted to see his new place where they would get to sleep sometimes. Mia said no. I suggested that it would be a good place for skating around in socks because there wasn't much furniture yet, so she switched to yes. "Do we have to?" Charlie asked, still not looking at his dad. "Of course not, Charlie," Daddy said. "But I would like to show you." As tears spilled down his cheeks, Charlie clenched his jaw and nodded his assent, like a man.

Soon they were both leaping at any chance to stay at Ted's place. I noted with no little resentment that by removing himself from our house, Dad had become a scarce and valuable commodity, while I was still same old, same old Mom. I had felt this even before our separation. Ted is a less accessible personality, the pursued rather than the pursuer in any intimate relationship. And I had been told by many adoption counselors that adopted kids have a natural tendency to chase after love that seems just out of reach. Furthermore, Ted is without rival as a paternal figure. Charlie's and Mia's birth dads figured in heavily when decisions were being made about who would parent their children, but both faded completely from our lives thereafter. I corresponded with Charlie's birth dad's mother for some time, but my last two Christmas cards came back marked "address unknown." And I've tried calling Mia's birth dad since she began asking at age ten to have some contact with him, but he's never answered my messages.

So Ted enjoys a starring role, without understudy or backup of any kind. By the time he moved out, I had definitely lost my taste (if I'd ever possessed it) for helping convince the kids that he was perfect in the part. But galling as it might be after the separation, I felt an acute need to pump him up. The kids needed him to be great now more than ever. So, damn it, I was going to cheerlead my runaway husband all the way into the Dads' Hall of Fame.

Meanwhile, there were our kids' other moms to consider. I had remained close to Angel and Angie in the years since they were compelled by circumstance to entrust their babies to us. Twenty-five-year-old Angie, who was just fourteen when Mia was born, and whose own mother had been murdered when she was ten, openly regards me as a maternal figure—for her, as well as her daughter. When Angie got married in 2001, Mia was the flower girl and I filled the bill as mother of the bride. Angel, on the other hand, has two boys, one and two years older than Charlie. I am now fifty-four, eighteen years her senior, yet I still occasionally look to her for tips on raising sons. This matrix of maternal ties made it terrifying to do what I needed to do next: tell them.

More than a year into our ordeal, I confessed to Angel and Angie, both of whom had expressly sought a two-parent family for their offspring, that I had failed to keep a dad on the premises. I told them I was going to sell our big, beautiful Victorian house and find a more modest abode. I reached out to these much younger women for their acceptance of me as another struggling single mom. Their reaction was empathetic and supportive. Both professed undying solidarity. Yet I worried that their faith in me was shaken. All of us became caught up in the need to renew and strengthen our connections. Angel sent her boys up from Texas to visit Charlie at our new house (Ted graciously footed the bill). I hosted Angie and her new husband and son when they drove down from Michigan (Ted joined us for dinners and a ferry trip to the Statue of Liberty). We *are* all still in this together, I realized—and so, I hoped, did our kids.

Still, the storm was fierce. Charlie's third-grade teacher called me one afternoon to say he had suddenly broken down crying on her shoulder after she'd pressed him to stop bothering a classmate. "My dad moved out," he told her. "I don't think he cares about me anymore." Everybody pulled out all the stops to persuade him this was not so, but his fears and his acting out continued sporadically at school.

Things grew even graver in Charlie's mind when Ted, a year after moving out, let the kids know about his love life. After informing me he was going to do it, he introduced his girlfriend—a professional in her thirties, beautiful, and childless by choice—and began trying to integrate her into their lives. Charlie resisted strenuously. Okay, I admit it; his mother pretty much did the same. I found it nearly unbearable that my husband's girlfriend could now be *in loco parentis* to my children, when they were merely postmarital baggage to her.

And there was the prickly problem of sex. My resentment of Ted's paramour figured in, of course. But kid issues also loomed large. Charlie was interested in girls by fourth grade, and was already talking about who "hooked up" and who "dumped" whom. I was frustrated that he wasn't getting a stronger role model for romance, one that involved commitment and caring for children. And Mia. She was born when her birth mom was just beginning ninth grade. We had emphasized since the cradle that she needed to be extremely careful about sexual behavior when she got older. Yet a day before Ted was to take Charlie and Mia to his girlfriend's beachfront digs for a vacation, he let slip that the kids would be staying in one room—and he and his lover would be together in another. I immediately put things on hold, which upset Ted greatly, but he ceded authority to me. For twelve hours straight, I agonized about which was the better choice: putting Charlie and Mia in an awkward position, or putting Ted in the awkward position and having to explain why to our kids. I let them go. Ted's girlfriend wrote me a note of thanks (Yechh!). And typically, Mia came home bubbly about the shore and the girlfriend's little dog, while Charlie returned down-in-the-mouth and feeling shunted aside.

Soon after, Charlie came into my home office as I was writing a private e-mail to a friend. When I tried to shield it from his view with my shoulder, he instantly demanded to know if I was going to get a boyfriend. "Dad promised me when he moved out that he wouldn't get a girlfriend," he said, "and then he did." I said it was unlikely, and that I had no plans or thoughts about it. "But," I added, "you never know what might happen." He glowered at me and stomped off.

My son's next school year, his last in elementary school, was extremely rocky. For one thing, by then I was in treatment for breast cancer, which sapped my energy and my sense of competency for a time. (I'm A-OK now.) Charlie responded by trying to cloak himself in tough-guy armor. He took to gelling his hair in wild colors and styles, and proclaimed a new public persona: "Outcast." My beloved Rebel Boy became the sworn enemy of a classmate who had once been his friend. "He always has to be so perfect," Charlie griped to me. "He's the perfect child with the perfect family and perfect grades, and he even has to play the piano perfectly. I'm thinking about how to commit the perfect murder."

Dad and his girlfriend, meanwhile, became practicing Buddhists, and occasionally took Charlie and Mia to their temple in New York for children's events replete with exultations of loving kindness. But their path seemed to bring our son no solace. He was not ready to look for ways to heal. After his graduation from fifth grade, I read the journal he'd kept that year at school. "The biggest shock of my life," he wrote in an early entry, "was when my dad got a girlfriend. First my birth mom leaves me—and then my dad."

By the time I read those words, Ted and his girlfriend were already finished. Ted never provided the details (certainly not to me), but he did make it plain that she wanted a partner whose life did not revolve around his children. When Ted told Charlie and Mia about the breakup, they were neither elated nor upset, just relieved to be back front-and-center. A few months later, Ted took a monthlong tour of sacred sites in Tibet, and a new woman, Susan, came into his life. This time, he kept quiet about his new relationship until it was on solid footing. But she lived in California. When Dad started being away a lot again, it slowly became apparent to everyone what was happening.

Once in a while, Susan came to visit Ted at his house in the next town over from ours, leaving her twins, who were three years younger than Mia, with her ex-husband and his new wife. One time, when Ted came over to pick up the kids, he brought Susan to meet me. I liked her immediately. Ted was approaching fifty at the time, and she was in her late thirties—wholesomely pretty and charmingly low-key. I could see from the way she greeted our kids that her mom skills were high-caliber. It took Charlie months to accept that Dad had another girlfriend. But he did eventually learn to relax in her presence, maybe because I led the way.

During this period, we followed a court-approved custody arrangement that kept the kids with me most school nights, and with Ted one or two nights, depending on his work schedule; on weekends, we generally alternated. Occasionally, we gave Mia and Charlie some choice in the matter, but that seemed to trigger more uncertainty and confusion. The question inevitably arose: If Dad has a home, and Mom has a home, which one is their "real" home? They already had to deal with questions about who their "real" parents were, raised by unwitting classmates and dimwit adults. Now even the question of where they lived was open to debate. Sometimes our theatrical daughter would stage a passion play on my doorstep: Just as she and Ted were about to leave, Mia would begin weeping and whining. "I don't know whether I want to stay at yours or go to his. What should I do, Mommy?" One evening Charlie got into an argument with his dad and walked three miles through a bad section of town in the dark to get to my house. "Are you saying I can't come home when I want to?" he hollered at me. Ted, who'd been frantic, rushed over, and both of us hugged our boy hard. We told him that no matter whom he was with, he had to stay put and work things out—not run to the other.

That summer, Susan came for a long visit and brought her kids for the first few weeks. Just as Susan's twins departed to be with their dad, Angie and her husband and son (whom we refer to as Mia's brother) arrived from Michigan for what has become an annual visit. Ted quickly suggested we all go to the Fourth of July concert in the park together. Angie, who seemed a bit leery of socializing with Ted's girlfriend, pulled me aside to ask if I really wanted to do it before okaying the plan. At the park, I could sense her irritation when her five-year-old climbed into Susan's lap and stayed put for much of the night. Still, as I lay on the blanket next to Angie, watching the three kids play, I wondered: Given our situation, could this be as good as it gets?

About six months later, Ted and Susan broke up. The long-distance thing was too wearing, and neither could bear to move their children away from their other parent, or bear to be away from their own kids for most of the year.

Now Ted has a new girlfriend of six months, age thirty. She is six years younger than Charlie's birth mom, and closer in age to him than to Ted. I've learned to live very well with birth moms who could be my daughters. But a potential stepmom who fills that bill? No way this goes down easy. This time, Charlie and Mia are the ones who seem to be leading the way to acceptance. While I still have the sense that my bringing home a serious boyfriend would cause an emotional ruckus, they have grown accustomed to Dad's serial-monogamist routine. Mia enjoys the new young woman, who gives her tips on where to buy tight jeans and lets her ride in her Porsche. Meanwhile, Charlie has his own girlfriend, and these days that is the relationship that matters most to him. When he went to camp for six weeks this past summer, he stayed true to his hometown girl—in much the way his dad has stayed true to his kids, whether they are physically with him or not.

Apparently my kids were the ones to see it first, but now, I do truly see it too: Ted left me; he didn't leave them. I am no longer wondering. I'm certain. This, I now know, *is* as good as it gets.

Keeping It
All in the Family

BOB SHACOCHIS

In 1995, about the same time my wife C and I decided to attempt in vitro fertilization, my niece Samantha received a terrifying announcement for her eighth birthday—her mother, Fran, C's older sister, had been diagnosed with an aggressive form of breast cancer. Prognosis: bleak. One year later, C returned from a visit with her sister on the West Coast with a question that, from my perspective, she didn't need to ask. Fran wanted to know how we felt about Samantha coming to live with us. "If Fran dies," my wife asked, "would you be willing for us to take Samantha?" Given the convergence of our two sets of circumstances, the tragic implications were too enormous to consider; it seemed as if we were suddenly horsetrading with God. But my answer was, and could only be, yes.

It was what Fran wanted, said my wife, visibly relieved. Families taking in their own, families absorbing those among them in need—it was the most central tenet in the contract of blood, the ties that bind. The sisters' own father, abandoned by his father, his mother unable to care for him, had been taken in and raised by a beloved uncle and aunt during the Great Depression, an act of compassion and generosity that would one day circle back to Samantha in ways she never could have imagined.

At the time, I had only a vague sense of Fran's loving but volatile, free-form relationship with her daughter, whom she carelessly regarded as an equal, sharing with Samantha everything: her bed since the time Samantha was in diapers, and especially after her husband was no longer welcome in it; the complex details of both her illness and her tempestuous marriage; even (I would learn) her husband's adults-only movie collection. I also knew that Fran and her husband, Sam, were a bit kinky as couples go, favoring a habit of reckless promiscuity that would eventually undo their marriage. When I asked C how Sam felt about the prospect of Samantha coming to live with us in Florida, I was told that he didn't feel his lifestyle was well suited for being the single parent of a little girl. He had acquiesced to Fran's judgment, or maybe he simply didn't want to argue with her anymore. I honestly don't know.

At any rate, there the issue lay, a tacit agreement between sisters, unspoken of for the next two years. Fran's breast cancer, after a radical mastectomy, massive chemotherapy and radiation treatments, and finally a stem cell transplant, refused to go into remission. Samantha was often abandoned in emergency rooms, alone and quietly crying in the waiting area, until her father, a law enforcement officer, got off work and rescued her.

C, meanwhile, on her third in vitro attempt to conceive, was pronounced permanently infertile. In the spring of 1998, our grief dispersed into a haze and we began to explore adoption in Lithuania. Ideally, we wanted to adopt one kid, a daughter, preferably newborn, although we had decided we would accept a child as old as four. Instead, a year later, we were improbably offered a sibling group, three brothers, ranging in age from three to eleven. We thought of ourselves as candidates for parenthood, not sainthood, and declined.

During that same spring of 1998, Fran made up her mind to leave her husband and move from San Francisco to Florida with Samantha, who had just turned eleven. C rented them a cottage down the street from our house in Tallahassee and began to acquaint herself with the regional cancer clinics. The day before Fran and Samantha planned to fly East, Fran, crippled by severe migraines, grabbed her daughter and drove to the emergency room. Three days later, on Mother's Day, I answered the phone and heard Fran on the other end, sobbing. The cancer had marched into her brain. She would not be moving to Florida. She would not be divorcing her husband after all.

Three months after that call, Fran would be dead. Two weeks later, C and I had Samantha, a *de facto* daughter. While nature and science and bureaucracy had failed to make us parents, tragedy persevered, and tragedy succeeded.

nter Samantha, center stage. Enter onto the periphery Ali, Samantha's half-sister, Fran's out-of-wedlock daughter whom she had given up for adoption at birth, twenty-eight years earlier. (After Ali's adoptive parents had threatened to disown her if she went searching for her biological mother, Ali found Fran—an event that filled her dying mother with inestimable joy—only to lose her again two years later.) Enter my wife, the favorite aunt, spiritually mauled by infertility. Enter me, perplexed. Do I now have a daughter? Perhaps two? Yes? No? In any case, I suddenly found myself the patriarch of a family that most resembled a storm-tossed life raft, its jury-rigged sails filled with the winds of loss and mourning. Our ability to navigate the domestic shoals was about to be severely tested.

On the surface, what was different was what you might expect: rearranging our schedules to drop off and pick up a sixth-grader at school, stocking the fridge with microwave pizzas, hosting sleepover parties with a houseful of giggling prepubescent girls, wrestling with the mighty homework-versus-TV controversy, nagging Samantha about hygiene. The laundry, in its volume and anthropological richness, was way different.

But the superficial gloss of normalcy couldn't mask the fact that Samantha was a profoundly traumatized child. What Samantha wanted from C was impossible, a blithe reenactment of the relationship they had always cherished: favorite aunt, favorite niece. By the simple fact of trying to be a mother, C spoiled the illusion and mutated, in the eyes of Samantha, from chaperone-of-choice to horrible mother. Samantha hated her for not being Fran. Similarly, for C, Samantha's blameless presence was a bleeding reminder she would never have her own biological child, and scraped at the wound that was Fran's death. From the minute Samantha unpacked into her new life, the psychic polarity between Samantha and my wife began to use up a lot of oxygen in the house.

Suddenly C woke up one morning to discover she was leading her sister's life, dealing with Fran's husband, Fran's child, Fran's problems. Her own life was being subsumed by a surrogate husband with whom every conversation devolved into a confrontation about child support and Sam's increasingly detached relationship with Samantha; a surrogate daughter crudely shaped by a sensibility radically different from ours; a real husband who had begun to show discouraging signs of alarm and disapproval that his wife wasn't who she had been, easygoing, good-humored, and optimistic.

The refrain, sung every day—"You are wanted here, wanted very much"—was filtered and muted by Samantha's malformed sense of the family unit. The truth was, although Samantha had lost a mother, she had entered into a familial environment that was more secure and affectionate than any life she would have obtained otherwise. She didn't know how to function with parents who loved each other and actually had a future. But she did, with the instinct of an only child, know how to triangulate. Samantha performed her calculations with a vengeance. At school and at home, every relationship was a *ménage à trois,* with Samantha and some-body else teamed up against the other person. Within three months, she was setting off, as it were, bedside bombs.

Samantha, unknowingly, brought an inhibition into the house, accelerating the inevitable decline of our sexual inti-macy that had started with the devastation of infertility (and would take several years to rebuild). Which is another way of saying we were brand-new parents and hadn't yet grown accustomed, and never really would, to making love with a kid in the house. Bumping up against that inhibition was the disconcerting level of sexual exposure and false sophis-tication Samantha carried with her from her life as a sushi-eating metro-girl in San Francisco. Given to watching movies with sexually explicit content, then concocting bedroom fantasies about C and me, Samantha poured hallucinatory erotic vignettes into her diary—fantasies that could poten-tially land us in very hot legal water and catapult Samantha into a tar pit of foster care if she shared her shocking imag-ination beyond the page.

Early that autumn of 1998, with my wife out of town on a business trip, I spent my first days and nights alone with Samantha, delighted to at least be able to pretend I had achieved the status of daddy. That first afternoon, I opened the door to her classroom and, with the questioning eyes of the teacher on me, announced, "I'm here to collect my daughter." I didn't know what else to say to preempt a com-plicated discussion of our relationship. Samantha, though, was not unaware of the psychological nuances and social conveniences of word choice.

"So, Samantha," I said cautiously once we were in my pickup truck, "back at school, when I called you my daughter, was that okay?"

"Yeah, that's fine."

"I don't really know what you're supposed to call me, besides Bob. I know I'm not your father, but you can call me Dad if you want."

"I already have a dad," she said. "I'll just call you my uncle."

"Of course," I answered. "Whatever you want to call me is fine, sweetheart." But within a year this naming of me would change, according to the situation: "parent" at school, "uncle" with friends, "Dad" when she wasn't paying attention and perhaps her heart spoke inadvertently, uncensored by confusion.

That first autumn, our roles and parental identities seemed to curdle into stereotypes. I was the good-time Charlie, the frivolous male, the bystander who could be co-opted as a witness for the defense; C was the disciplinarian, the overextended female, trapped by the solemn duty of blood and betrayed in ways both subtle and overt by her partner. Quickly, C came to believe she was being deliberately excluded, even to the extent of feeling physically deprived, when I tickled the kid. "She gets the playfulness now, instead of me," C lamented one day. It shocked me to realize she was right.

We were green parents, but Samantha was a veteran child. Yes, you can stay up a half hour more, I'd tell Samantha, not realizing she'd already petitioned C and the answer had been no. We hadn't been given eleven years to discern how she ticked, to map the contours of her personality, to crack the code on how best to deal with her, to know how to love her. No matter what. C slowly began to resent her loss of free time and her extreme loss of privacy; in her unhappiness she unreasonably condemned herself for failing as a mother. I, no less unfairly, resented my wife's inability to climb out of the dark, dark place she had fallen into after the failure of IVF; her quickness to take the child's transgressions, innocent or calculated, personally; her incapacity to recover her former lightness of being.

We had wanted a child, we had gotten a child, and it was a royal mess.

How do you put the love back in a young girl's life when the love, in its blooming tenderness, has been uprooted from her heart? How do you restore her faith in love, her trust in others? On Samantha's twelfth birthday, I sat on the bathroom floor cradling her in my arms, waiting for her tears to dry, waiting for her to unburden herself, telling her she was safe—in our house, in our lives, in my arms.

"This isn't supposed to be my life," she finally blurted.

No, honey, I had to tell her. This is supposed to be your life. And our life, too. But even then I had begun to have my doubts about the healing power of love, a Band-Aid we kept applying to Samantha's lacerated soul. Sometimes it would stick for weeks, sometimes less than a day. Off it would come, and we'd put it on again. Off, on. Off, on. Off.

During those sweet times when it stuck, Samantha was charming, obedient, respectful, when she wanted to be; prompt, composed, and not least of all, fun. She would, as time went on, retire to bed each evening with a book. My wife introduced her to Nancy Drew (who, you might recall, had lost her mother), which Samantha devoured, until Nancy was booted out by Ursula Le Guin and Harry Potter (who also lost a mother). We took her and Ali overseas on Christmas holidays, bought her most of what she wanted—clothes, computer, her own telephone line—and let her make her own choices about most things.

That freedom included letting her decide the precise nature of her relationship with us, which hibernated in legal murk. Her father Sam in San Francisco had granted us custody but not guardianship. Technically, we had no rights over the child, unable even to allow an emergency room doctor to lay a hand on her. Her fading bond with her father was a source of pain and confusion for her: Do you love him, Samantha? Yes. Do you want to be with him? No. Would you like us to try to formally adopt you? Yes.

But then we'd gently explain that if her father resisted the adoption, she herself might have to go before a judge in a courtroom, and he might ask her to make a choice. Samantha didn't want to do that, didn't want to hurt her father by rejecting him in public. Yet simultaneously she pleaded with us never to send her back to him, a possibility that became an issue when it was time, after a childhood spent in private schools, for Samantha to enter public high school in Tallahassee. Sam—the three of us by now referred to him as Big Daddy—balked at the idea of signing over Samantha's legal guardianship to us. But the public schools in Florida wouldn't admit a student who didn't reside with either her natural parents or certified guardians. The summer between middle school and Samantha's freshman year in high school dragged on with no response from San Francisco. Days before the enrollment deadline, we issued an ultimatum: Transfer guardianship, or Samantha's on a plane tomorrow. Sam didn't know we had no intention of following through on the threat; the matter was expeditiously resolved.

We never spoke ill of Sam in front of Samantha—Fran had done more than enough of that—and made a point of doing what little we could to shield Samantha's image of her father from further corruption. But it wasn't easy, given Big Daddy's continuing refusal to release a nickel of child support without first exacting the price of an hour-long quarrel. When I suggested to C that the emotional cost of those monthly checks was too high, that we could manage the expense of raising his daughter, she was searingly opposed to letting him off the hook. The money, if nothing else, prevented him from ignoring Samantha completely.

As it was, Sam's infrequent phone conversations with Samantha were short and monosyllabic. The first Thanksgiving she spent with us, Big Daddy flew into town, and I took him straight from the airport to school to pick up his child. When the reunion between them inspired no embrace, I felt obliged to prod Samantha into hugging him, which she accomplished with stiff reluctance and no kiss forthcoming (a familiar sad scene to me, since my wife and Samantha recreated it regularly). After that visit, Sam never came out East again. Samantha's first trip back to San Francisco that summer overlapped with a cruise Big Daddy had planned with his new girlfriend. He wouldn't reschedule. Instead, he

arranged for the parents of Samantha's grade-school best
friend to collect her at the airport, and did not change the
plan when, the day before Samantha's arrival, the friend's
father died of cancer. Samantha spent the week of the cruise
in camp, then a few awkward days with Sam and his girlfriend; then she came back to us, battered anew in ways we
couldn't know.

Toward the end of her freshman year of high school,
Samantha posted a screed on a student website on the
Internet that excoriated my wife for being a self-centered
bitch and falsely (and dangerously) accused me of being an
abusive monster who beat her black-and-blue. Stunned and
furious, I asked her, "Don't you believe we love you?"

"Come on, Bob," she answered. "I know you and C love
me. But you know about my life. I can't love anybody. I just
can't do it. I'm incapable of love."

She was fifteen years old, and I believed her, or rather,
I believed in the whipsawed barrenness of her shattered
heart.

That summer while spending her annual week at a lake
in Virginia with C's cousin, his Swiss wife, and their three
children, Samantha listened avidly as the cousin suggested
she spend a year abroad at their home in Luxembourg, studying at the renowned international high school where he
taught. The following March, the phone rang—the cousin
calling from Luxembourg to say how delighted he and his
family were that Samantha would be coming to live with them
in Europe the following year and spend her sophomore year

at the International School. Excuse me? Behind our backs, Samantha had found herself a new family. After my wife straightened out the misunderstanding with her cousin, we told Samantha that she was still too young and immature to be foisted off on another family, but if she kept up her grades, improved her attitude, and showed a little more responsibility, she could choose to go abroad for her junior year, if that's what she wanted. Yes, she said, she did.

But she did little to prove it. Throughout her sophomore year, Samantha's fuse burned ever shorter. When the detonation came, it was worse than C and I had imagined. The irony was that, by that point, Samantha was happier, more invested in her sense of home, more comfortable and at ease with her life than she had ever been before. She finally believed she was where she belonged, and in the confidence of that awareness, knew she could act up and the consequence would be normal, predictable. Her parents would get mad but they weren't going to, like, give her away or anything, right?

The gateway to this newfound sense of belonging was, as it always is, friends. After almost five years in Tallahassee Samantha had finally found her crowd, and they were hell on wheels attached to rocket boosters. Drugs, sex, (bad) rock and roll. Yippee. Her grades fell, her head drained by an obsession with cool and its risky, seductive edges. Our patience lasted right up to the night she was busted for marijuana, when I shouted witheringly, grounded Samantha until spring break, and, until further notice, took everything out of her room—television, cell phone and land line, e-mail, IM, chat rooms—that had made it her sanctuary.

Up until this moment, Samantha had remained so ex-
cited about spending her junior year abroad that the cousin
and my wife, on their respective sides of the Atlantic, had
initiated the administrative process to make it happen. Now
Samantha began to have second thoughts. Suddenly she
loved Florida more than anyplace on earth, and her friends,
well, they were so fuckin' cool, how could she ever leave
them? C and I, who had signed on to the once-in-a-lifetime
opportunity with a sense of loss, now had a change of heart
ourselves. We had lost control of Samantha. A year in Europe, we became convinced, was a necessary intervention
for her survival. When her father concurred, we gave the
Luxembourg branch of the family a cautionary heads-up—
troubled kid ahead—and the deal was sealed.

The cousin had known Samantha most of her life and,
of equal significance, had known Samantha's extended Virginia family all of his life. It was his grandparents, my wife's
great-uncle and great-aunt, who had taken in and raised
Samantha's maternal grandfather during the Depression. The
cousin was a dedicated educator at one of the best private
high schools in Europe; like us, he imagined a genuine opportunity, academically and culturally, for Samantha, if she
accepted his invitation to study abroad for at least one year,
and why not two? But there was a transcendent and deeply
personal sense of altruism to his offer as well, an impulse to
echo, as his grandparents had, as we had, the familial obli-
gation to not turn away from your own, to gather in and
shelter any child in need. She's family and you don't give up
on family, he e-mailed to us that November, even if they
really piss you off sometimes.

Unfortunately, and despite the fact that he and his wife were, unlike us, seasoned parents who were successfully raising three teenagers, Samantha behaved no differently in their house from the way she had in ours. Samantha was a divide-and-conquer kid, he wrote to us in Florida. Though united with his wife on how to respond to Samantha's challenges, he, like my wife before him, felt trapped into the role of bad cop. By the end of the school year the cousin threw in the towel; there would be no invitation to stay a second year. "It is not you and it is not me. It is simply Samantha," he e-mailed C. "I can't help but feel like a failure to her but I can't risk hurting my own family any more than I have."

Despite Samantha's dismal domestic performance, her year in Luxembourg did not pass without achievement and growth. After she volunteered to participate in a Global Issues Project at her school, her social conscience awakened; she began attending conferences throughout Europe, working in a group responsible for addressing the problem of infectious diseases, heading an initiative to raise money for breast cancer research. From Europe, she phoned to tell us that though she was homesick for Florida, she sincerely wanted to complete her high school education in an international baccalaureate program similar to the one in Luxembourg.

Her grades were good enough for the challenging curriculum, but when we discovered Tallahassee offered no such program, an Internet search turned up a tenuous alternative: a private school in San Francisco. To qualify for enrollment, she would have to repeat her junior year. Did she want us to broach the subject with her father?

Yes.

Last month, C and I saw Samantha for the first time in a year when she flew into New Mexico from San Francisco, where, at seventeen, she now lives with her father and his girlfriend. At the airport in Albuquerque, she looked radiant when she saw me, running to hug me tighter and longer than she ever had before, repeating the scene with C two hours later, up in the mountains at our cabin. The next day Samantha and I left to stake out a campsite in the high country, Latir Lakes, for a large family reunion of relatives from Virginia, Colorado, and Maryland that would include Ali and her fiancé from New York City.

By the time we pitched our tent, the weather had changed. Three successive squalls pummeled us far into the night, so we huddled in the tent, played gin rummy, and talked. About living with her father (surprisingly positive) and his girlfriend (unexpectedly negative), about the cousin (predictably vitriolic) and Europe (a different moral and political reality). Samantha seemed more mature to me, so I asked how her year in Luxembourg had changed her. She responded that she was more realistic, more responsible, less impatient, more caring, less wild. "I'm not like I was in Tallahassee," she assured me. "I'm not that person anymore, Bob."

That night, as the rain roared against our tent, I lay beside my once-upon-a-time daughter as she snored softly, cherishing the memory of my many firsts with her: teaching her how to fish and ski in these mountains, swim and snorkel in Florida; trying to teach her how to shuck an oyster, drive

a car, the comedy of trying to help her buy her first bra; trying to teach her to be kind, to be decent, to be loving.

As I drifted toward sleep, I remembered an argument
that I once had with a friend, to whom I was trying to explain how difficult it was to get the nomenclature right with
Samantha. C and I were her parents . . . but we weren't. We
were her on-loan, full-time, substitute mom and dad, but of
course we were not her mother and father, and yet mothering and fathering were exactly what was required of us, and
the language was always getting tangled up in fickleness and
sanctimony.

"You're just her aunt and her uncle," she responded. "You
will never be her parents. Never."

All these years later, I still feel a deep anger stir remembering my (former) friend's narrow and unfruitful line of
reasoning. If we had adopted Samantha from Lithuania,
who would be offended if she called us Mom and Dad? If
we aren't her parents, then would somebody please tell her
parents to come and get her?

Yet after taking parenthood on a six-year-long test drive,
I confess I'm unsure what to make of it all. I still ache for
the child C and I will never have. But I miss Samantha, too;
like C, I look into the hole she left in our lives, and sigh.

In one month's time, I'll dress in a tuxedo to walk Ali
down the aisle to marry Christof, the man with whom she
has chosen to spend her life. C will be in the wedding, too,
number-one bridesmaid and honorary mother, and of course
Samantha, attending the bride, her sister who fell from the
sky. I expect to be called upon to toast the mishmash of

postmodern family building of which I and my wife are the unwitting architects. I will also toast Christof's absent father, whose ashes lie in the lake beside which he and Ali will exchange vows. Which brings to mind an insight by the Canadian novelist Robertson Davies: that sometimes a person has, in the course of his or her life, many fathers, and the truth might be that in the final measure the biological one is the least influential or significant of them all.

Well Cheers.

On the otherwise bare wall in the chamber of my heart reserved for the ornaments of parenthood hangs a Father's Day card. I love you, Dad, it says, in a teenager's chirpy-looking scrawl. Signed, Samantha.

I don't imagine I'll ever get another. Still, I know that at the moment she signed that card, Samantha meant it. I know that when she is most real and true to herself, she does in fact, despite her own disclaimer, know how to love, and how to express that love, to C, to me, to whoever has earned it. Not just to take it and let it hurt, but to give it and let it shine.

In our hearts, endlessly broken, endlessly filled.

♥

FOUR

Personal
Transformations

Reluctant No More
(Not That I Ever Was)

JOE TREEN

When my wife and I adopted our daughter in China, the expression most frequently used to describe me was "dragged kicking and screaming all the way." I still hear this every once in a while, usually *sotto voce* from the next room, and, of course, it is an out-and-out lie. I was not dragged. I did not kick. Maybe I screamed a little but that was *before* we got on the plane. On the way over I was a model passenger, quiet as a mouse. This is the kind of misrepresentation I have suffered at the hands of my wife and other adoption fanatics who have maliciously labeled me The Reluctant Spouse (a phrase cruelly concocted by my wife that has somehow found its way into popular usage).

My wife even wrote a book in 1997 about our adoption

(a book she called *An Empty Lap* and I called, behind her back, at first, *I Married an Asshole*) in which she includes all sorts of lies, fibs, distortions, falsehoods, untruths, fabrications, misrepresentations, libels, prevarications, tall tales, fish stories, and Texas-sized whoppers about my mental processes leading up to the adoption of our daughter.

It is not true, for example, that I demanded a divorce on multiple occasions. I am certain that happened only two or three times. And not to belabor a point, but I did not try to put our then-new house up for sale one morning after a particularly bad commute on the bus that left me angry and furious and ready to blow up New Jersey Transit headquarters, a crime that surely would have gone unpunished given the circumstances on Route 3 that day. I simply called our realtor to inquire about the housing market. Idle curiosity. Nothing more.

Not until the final chapters of my wife's so-called memoir is it suddenly revealed—*deus ex machina*—that none of the terrible and dire things she spends several hundred pages predicting actually came true. She buries the good news at the end. I didn't run off. I didn't get a divorce. I didn't sell the house. I changed diapers. I gave baths. I fed. I memorized *Goodnight Moon*. I went to Pokemon movies on Saturday afternoons. I stayed home from work so I could pitch in at the co-op nursery. I videotaped an extraordinary number of recitals and concerts and elementary school plays, during which I fretted about our daughter's tendency to wind up in the back row behind much taller and far less talented children. I helped with homework and class projects. I dropped off and picked up. I set reasonable rules, like no ear piercing or dating until she turns forty.

So what happened? How did I go from ever-so-slightly cautious about adoption to second assistant coach of my daughter's softball team? How did I make the transition from understated apprehension to card-carrying member of Indian Princesses, a father-daughter organization rumored to be invented by mothers so they could have time for themselves? What can I say? I fell for the kid. Somehow I became a father.

There is a debate in our family as to when this occurred. My wife insists I was hooked about thirty seconds after the ladies from the orphanage first brought Becky into our hotel room in Yangzhou that January afternoon in 1995. I know this isn't true. First of all, I couldn't get near her. The Chinese officials handed Becky over to my wife and my wife wasn't letting go. Then the entire female staff of the hotel showed up to take a look and pass her around. Lastly, other families traveling with us came trooping into the hotel room with their newly acquired babies. It was a zoo. Crowds of people. I was out in the hall with the other fathers.

Later that night, however, everyone had gone. My wife was asleep. And Becky—in a makeshift crib on the floor between our beds—was making strange sounds. It wasn't crying. It wasn't moaning either. She was also gesturing oddly with her hands. I took her out in the hall and walked up and down as I tried to get her to go back to sleep. But she kept making the sound and rubbing her hands together.

Suddenly, it dawned on me. This child is hungry. This

child needs food. And then a certain panic: That means I have to feed her—no easy task, considering I didn't have a clue how. I mean, I did know there were these containers of soy-based powdered milk that you mixed with water. But then I discovered that you had to take these little plastic bags and put them inside these little plastic bottlelike cylinders and then put the right amount of powdered milk into the plastic bag and then pour in boiling hot water from a thermos and then cool it off because any idiot, including me, knows that boiling hot water is too hot to drink, especially if you are seven months old. And then you had to screw a lid on top. And you had to do all of this in a cramped hotel bathroom using only one hand because there is this child in the other hand. And you had to do it quietly because your wife is sleeping. And you had to do it quickly because the child is hungry. And you had to do it carefully because pouring boiling hot water on a seven-month-old is not recommended.

I solemnly pledged that night that I would, right then and there, return to the United States and personally murder the head of the Playtex corporation for creating a product that was impossibly difficult to use when you didn't know how to use it. But there was still the matter of this cute little girl who was looking up at me, moaning a strange little moan, rubbing her hands in an odd little way, expecting me to be an adult and not climb on the next airplane and not kill the president of Playtex but rather work it out and feed her. And so I did.

That's when it happened. I sat on the edge of the bed and held this infant as she gobbled down food that I had made for her. Afterward, she fell asleep and I put her back in her makeshift crib and watched her for a while. I was hooked. Within a day or two, I had even forgiven Playtex. Those bottles were easy, second time out.

Now, anyone who knew me knew this would happen. Even I knew it would happen. Only my wife was in the dark. But that's not her fault; a lot of women don't get it. There is a reason men hesitate just a tiny little bit before plunging into adoption, a reason that is especially true for older men (I was in my early fifties) or for men who have already had children from a previous marriage (not my case, but I've known a lot of guys). Men are realists; they know what's at stake. It comes down to this: time, money, career, age, sleep, diapers, and control of the remote.

Where are you going to get time for a kid? You don't have any time as it is. If you had a kid, you wouldn't get to do anything—even go to the gym. No more spur-of-the-moment movies. No more dinners at your favorite restaurant. No more winter vacations to Caribbean islands with topless beaches.

And what about money? Children are expensive, especially if they wear clothes and eat food. (Let's not even talk about summer camps, orthodontics, or piano lessons.) When you reach sixty-five, there is every chance in the world that you will have retired and the kid will be in high school, looking at universities. *Expensive* universities. No community college for your kid; your kid will go to Harvard or Yale or Princeton! How are you going to afford the Ivy League when you've only just started to think about maybe saving for retirement? Do you really want to work at McDonald's in your golden years?

Then there's your career. You think some boss will put up with your having to stick to a schedule, having to go home at night to feed the baby instead of finishing important projects that he or she put off until the last minute? You'll get fired. You'll never find another job at your age. Not in this economy. You'll be out on the street with a wife and kid. How many homeless people send their children to Princeton?

Besides, you're too old for all this. Not too old to have put off saving for retirement but too old to have a child. You'll be exhausted getting up every two hours to feed a squalling baby or, worse, change a dirty diaper. Let's face it, you've got other things to do. Important things. With a kid, you'll never be allowed to do them—or anything else. You think you'll get to watch *Meet the Press* Sunday mornings when *Teletubbies* is on at the same time? You think NPR is an option in the car with Radio Disney beckoning at the other end of the dial? Think again.

And think about this: If this is going to be an adoption, we're not even talking about your own flesh and blood. The adoption crazies don't like to admit this, but we're talking about someone else's kid. Some Russian or Asian kid. Didn't we struggle against the Russians in the Cold War for half a century? Weren't we pretty much at war with one Asian country or another from Pearl Harbor to the fall of Saigon? Now we have to raise their children?

That's why a lot of men don't want to adopt. Their fears are not entirely groundless (bad news about the remote). Men can see this. They can figure out the cons—oh, can they figure out the cons—but what they don't see ahead of time are the pros. They don't see the big picture until they actually have a child. And then they get it. They understand how fatherhood and adoption enrich their lives and all that other junk men don't like to talk about. It's like marriage. My wife and her cronies say I was dragged down the aisle kicking and screaming, which we all know is another big fat lie (I didn't even walk down the aisle, I stood at the front). But now that I've been married for a while, it's terrific. My wife is perfect in every way. (Hi, honey.)

So what are the pros? How can adoption be worth it? Let's not waste time on all the gushy love stuff. Let's get to something important: career. I think Becky actually helped. Since her arrival, I have moved from the middle of magazine mastheads to near the very top. Bosses like the idea that you have children; it means you can't afford to quit no matter how awful the bosses get. Or maybe they just like children. For reasons I can no longer remember, I had to take Becky to the office at one point when she was about three. Fortunately, my company had an emergency day care center for when normal child care falls through. Following protocol, I took Becky to the company cafeteria for lunch. Then I decided to take her up to my office. When we got off the elevator, my deputy, Sarah, came running up. The editor of the magazine I worked for wanted to see me right away. I tried to get Becky to stay with Sarah but she would have none of it. So, reluctantly, fearing the worst, I walked hand in hand with Becky to my boss's office. He was there with the editor of another magazine. The next thing I knew, my boss and Becky were dancing to music from the jukebox he kept in his office (don't ask) and the other editor was clapping along. I wasn't fired. I was a hero. I had a cute kid.

I got promoted. And that helped with money. (I figure we're all set. All we have to do is skip meals between 2012 and 2016, and Becky can go to any college she wants, no matter how expensive.) But a funny thing happened on the way to the top. Adopting Becky changed my priorities. Until she arrived, I had never really worried about spending too much time at the office or on the road. That was life. Now I had another life. I wanted to be home, not at work.

When Becky was five, I got a dream assignment: put out a special magazine issue on Vietnam. Initially, it meant a one-week trip to set things up. But a few weeks later I had to go back for a month to oversee the reporting and photography. This did not sit well with Becky. I don't know if abandonment issues that can come up with adoptees were at play here, but as I was putting her to bed a few nights before I was to leave, she told me she didn't want me to go. I told her I didn't want to go either but I had to because of my job. With that, she started shouting, "Vietnam is stupid, Daddy. Vietnam is stupid."

I left on a Halloween night. First I took her trick-or-treating and then a cab came to get me. She wouldn't even hug me good-bye. She ran off with a friend to get more candy. I don't think I fully pulled the knife out of my heart until the day I got back—in time to meet her school bus. Her shout of "Daddy!" as she jumped off the bus and ran toward me made up for everything.

The discovery that maybe Vietnam *is* stupid was not the only lesson I learned from adoption. Another has to do with age. I've noticed that a lot of men who adopt are older—or should I say "distinguished"?—like myself. Guess what? Kids make you young. You learn their life. Their music. Their schoolwork. Their movies. Their culture. Their concerns. Plus you stay out of trouble. Sledding with your daughter is a far less divorce-prone way to turn sixty than, say, buying a Porsche Boxster and having an affair.

But the really big lesson I learned is that adoption doesn't matter. Once you've become a parent, you stop thinking about how the kid came into your life. You're her father. She's your child. Topic A changes from host countries and adoption agencies to schools and summer camps. Adoption becomes a footnote, an asterisk that can easily be ignored. And ignore it I do.

So do other fathers who have adopted. I had lunch recently with journalist Mark Frankel (Nanjing, '95). He is brilliant, prone to great thoughts, as proven by the fact that he agrees with me entirely. "Adoption is not a state of being," he said over the priciest meal my expense account could bear. "You don't say your daughter '*is* adopted,' you say she '*was* adopted.'" In other words, adoption is an event. It is one way of many to create a family. After that, it is about as relevant as the C-section your neighbor had when she was creating hers.

This may be hard to believe if you are still trying to adopt. In March 2000 I was coming back from my final trip to Vietnam. On the plane from Ho Chi Minh City to Hong Kong was an American man in his thirties holding an infant Vietnamese boy on his lap. As I passed him on the way to the lavatory, I asked if he had just adopted. When he said that he had, I told him that my wife and I had done the same thing a few years earlier in China.

"It's great," I said.

"How long did it take to get a referral?" he asked.

My God. Process. I hadn't thought about the ordeal of adoption—the waiting, the changing rules, the crazy wringer they put you through—since we brought Becky home. This man was obviously still feeling it all.

"That's a long story," I said. "And a long time ago. Now she's just another suburban kid in New Jersey."

It is clear, though, that Becky thinks about her beginnings from time to time. But to me, this is just one more thing on the ever-growing list of things parents have to help their child come to grips with. Most parents have to explain such thorny issues as death, religion, the monster under the bed. My wife and I have all that—and adoption, too. Usually the subject comes up around her birthday, but recently we've been hearing about it at other times.

"What time were you born?" Becky asked me the other day.

"Six something in the morning," I said.

"What time was I born?"

I could have made up an answer, but my wife and I operate on the theory that it's best to be as open and honest as possible.

"I don't know," I said. "They didn't tell us that part."

She was not happy. "Erika knows and Ariana and Andrea and Alex. *Everybody*."

"Yeah, but none of them were born in China. You're special."

I don't know if she bought it or not. A few days later she was asking what would have happened to her if she hadn't been adopted by us. That she is asking questions doesn't mean much. She has always asked questions, starting before she could talk and she would point at things and say, "Dah?" And I would tell her what it was. After she could talk, the questions got more interesting: "Daddy, if you put your shoes on backwards can you still turn around?" or "Daddy, is Mother Nature married to God?" I notice she triangulates; she'll ask my wife and me the same thing to see if she gets the same answer.

One question Becky has not asked so far has been about her biological father. As nearly as I can tell, she has never had a single question about him. This could change, of course, especially when she becomes a teenager and I officially become the man who kidnapped her from what would have been a perfect life in Yangzhou. I figure he is just some guy in the middle of Jiangsu Province who got lucky sometime in September 1993. Orphanage officials told us Becky's biological mother was an unwed college student. They told us nothing about the father. It is entirely possible that he doesn't even know he had a child. That's okay with me. Truth be told, I'd prefer to think I'm the only father in the universe worrying about my daughter's future. That's one burden I'm not reluctant to shoulder solo.

And Then
Everything Changed

ADAM PERTMAN

First, my mother expressed her soaring joy. I had called to tell her that, minutes earlier, my wife and I had received the awesome news—the exquisite, exhilarating, palpitation-inducing news. A boy had been born in Colorado, his mother had chosen us as his new parents, and we were to pick him up within a few days. "*Mazel tov*, that's so wonderful," my mother said, her smile so intense that it was almost audible. Then, in her Polish-accented English, she offered one of her trademark off-the-cuff chestnuts, its wisdom so striking that it has stayed with me ever since: "All right," she said. "Now you can worry for the rest of your life."

Every parent, however he or she becomes a parent, experiences the essential truth of my mother's insight—from the moment we begin fretting about our kids' health and development as infants, through the continuum of anxiety about their performance and behavior in middle school, and on into the adult years, when we anguish about their professional and personal progress. The simple truth is that having children brings out a generally positive trait in most of us: a perpetual, selfless concern for another human being.

For better or worse, of course, that is only one item on a very long list of ways in which our sons and daughters alter our lives forever. Many parents, for instance, leave their careers to focus on child-rearing, a path chosen (much to her own surprise) by my wife, Judy Baumwoll. Or to help their kids medically, academically, or in some other way, parents become advocates for a cause. And because children compel their mothers and fathers to reevaluate their priorities and recalibrate their inner compasses, many parents find themselves rejecting, revising, or intensifying their answers to particular cultural, political, behavioral, or moral questions. But when Judy and I received that glorious call from Colorado just over a decade ago, I had not a glimmer of a clue that I would check off so many items on the list. I knew a child would rearrange my home life, but upend my career and worldview? Those two items weren't even on my list.

I don't think I gave adoption a second's thought until Judy and I, in our early forties, confronted the aching reality that we could not create a family the old-fashioned way. I was a happy, professionally satisfied, well-compensated journalist who thought he would continue doing what he'd been doing for nearly twenty years until the day he retired. I had developed a broad but not especially deep knowledge in lots of areas, and although I held strong private views on many issues, I didn't take public stands on virtually anything.

Today, it's all adoption, all the time.

As executive director of the nonprofit Evan B. Donaldson Adoption Institute, a preeminent national policy, research, and education organization, I have seen adoption become my job, my mission, my passion. I've learned more about its varied, complex issues than I ever imagined I would know about any single topic. Adoption is the focus of my research, my writing, my talks to reporters and conference audiences, indeed just about anyone who will listen. My opinions about its often-controversial components—from finding homes for children from foster care and orphanages to adoptees' right to access their own birth records—are as strong as those I've ever held on any subject. Many of my friends are now adoptive parents, birth parents, adopted adults, and adoption professionals. At home, adoption-related matters are a common topic of discussion, whether Judy and I are discussing a visit with the biological mother of one of our kids (Emmy, now eight, joined us three years after Zack, now eleven), figuring out what to do about a cutting remark one of their schoolmates has made about adoption, or just yakking at night about how lucky it was that we couldn't get Judy pregnant.

Most days, I revel in the realization that I will probably travel this singular path for the rest of my days. I certainly didn't see that coming in 1994, when I first asked my editors at the *Boston Globe* if I could write a series of stories about adoption. It took another three years, after a detour to the paper's California bureau, before they finally said yes. But from the start, with just the information from a couple of orientation sessions at the agency we used to adopt Zack, I quickly sensed it was a meaty, complicated, and nuanced subject—in other words, a good story.

What I did not think was that I wanted to write about adoption because it was about my family or for my child. The adoption process provided me with a glimpse into another world, but that didn't make the story more personal than one I might have stumbled upon if I'd discovered the police were using a new high-tech detection device to give me a speeding ticket. While I was often moved during interviews for my adoption series, I kept my emotional distance. I often felt elated or outraged or amazed, but my job was not to express those feelings; it was to figure out how best to let the hundreds of voices on my tape recorder speak for themselves. The six months I spent researching and writing my Adoption Revolution series proved the most challenging work I'd ever done. It was also the most rewarding.

I walked away with a newfound understanding, both conceptual and personal, that the institution has changed radically over the last few decades. Secrecy and shame, once the twin hallmarks of adoption, are being replaced with openness and pride. Adoptive parents, who are raising record numbers of children from other countries and from foster care, are literally and figuratively changing the complexion of our country's families. They are also changing the very definition of family, not only in the home but also in classrooms and communities across the land. In most domestic infant adoptions, for instance, the biological mother now chooses the new parents and increasingly maintains some level of relationship with the child she created. For Judy and me, this would prove the most eye-opening—and life-changing—notion of all.

The *Globe* series, which received greater attention than anything I'd ever written, led me to two new basic understandings. The first was that adoption is not a one-time event but rather, like marriage, an ongoing process with an array of lifelong effects. The second, that principally because of the stigmas and stereotypes that thrived during its secretive past, too many of the laws, policies, practices, and attitudes surrounding adoption remain outdated, ill-informed, and unfair. The "adoption revolution," I saw, is still a work in progress.

That understanding, though, did not compel me to alter significantly the focus of my work for the sake of my children. I absolutely loved them, of course. I meant it—as every parent does—when I said that I'd do anything in the world for them. But by that I meant things like helping them with homework or tending to aches and bad dreams in the middle of the night.

About a year after the *Globe* series appeared, I started to chase a more selfish dream: to write my first book. Mountains of interviews and information remained untouched in my notebooks. Moreover, I realized that for every detail I'd collected, there were four others I hadn't had time to pursue. A book had the potential to touch people's hearts; teach them about a part of their world they didn't know as much about as they thought they did (because it's very hard to learn about secrets); and, perhaps, help promote some positive changes.

I don't know how I could not have grasped the deeply personal nature of the project, but I honestly didn't. The early drafts of *Adoption Nation: How the Adoption Revolution Is Transforming America* barely mentioned the journey Judy and I had taken from infertility to adoption; how Zack and Emmy had come into our lives; what I'd felt and thought throughout the process. I added those elements only after my editor advised, "Everyone who reads your book will want to know your story, too, not just all those others you tell." The deliberate infusion of my family and sentiments led me not only to think very differently about my work but also to finally grasp the personal significance of what I was attempting to do. This was about my kids. I had stumbled on an opportunity to try to do for Zack and Emmy what all parents dream of: to leave the world a better place for their children.

Once that realization set in, everything changed.

I jettisoned all pretense of "straight" journalism, now believing I could more effectively serve my book's readers—and my kids—by playing the role of informed guide rather than detached observer. I found myself writing with more passion than I knew I had in me, especially when discussing aspects of adoption that could have a direct impact on Zack and Emmy. More daunting, I expanded my vision of *Adoption Nation*. No longer satisfied with my plan to paint the big picture about an extraordinary institution, I wanted this book also to be a vehicle for instigating change. I wanted to accelerate the pace of a revolution that most people weren't even aware was taking place. I know that sounds fanciful, or even pompous. Yet when I saw the kinds of things my kids would confront—well-intentioned but hurtful comments, negative portrayals of their lives on television and in movies, deep misunderstandings about their birth parents, laws that treated them as second-class citizens—it seemed utterly worth attempting.

After a one-year unpaid leave to write my book, I returned to the *Globe,* this time as the "family and children's issues" reporter. After *Adoption Nation* was published in late 2000, something new and awkward began to happen: Even as I was reporting adoption-related stories, I started receiving calls from other reporters seeking interviews for their own adoption-related stories. I also was receiving invitations to speak publicly; answering a nonstop stream of calls and e-mail from adoptive parents, birth parents, and adult adoptees; even getting messages from adoption practitioners saying they were rethinking some practice or policy or ethical stance because of what they'd read in my book.

For half a year, I functioned as both a reporter and an adoption expert. Though exhilarating and challenging, this labor-intensive dual career was ultimately untenable. I was advocating for children—but seeing less and less of my own. I also was traversing a tricky ethical tightrope as I offered public opinions on topics I was trying to write about objectively. I came to the conclusion that the only principled thing to do was to make a choice. So in June 2001, I left the profession that had been so good to me for a quarter-century. I didn't know exactly how I would provide for my family going forward, but I knew it would be something relating to adoption, something that would make a genuine difference for

Zack and Emmy and the millions of other Zacks and Emmys out there.

Judy and I were aware of the financial risks, but she never wavered. "You have to do this," she told me from the start. "You know you do." She was right, and I'll be forever grateful for her love and encouragement. She's not an adoption specialist, but she is a pro at loving and caring for her children, so her sentiments were rooted in a desire to improve their lives as well as to support her husband. Another important factor for both of us was that, by then, we had gotten over most of the insecurities we'd felt as preadoptive and early-adoptive parents. Our conversations had turned from wondering whether we'd done the right thing in agreeing only to exchange pictures and letters with Zack's and Emmy's birth mothers, to wishing we had contact with the women (and men) who'd blessed us with their children.

We have since reconnected with both of them, first with Emmy's birth mom, Erin, in California, when our daughter was four, then with Zack's birth mom, Angela, in Colorado, just a few months ago at this writing. The trickiest part of our extended family, at least so far, is juggling travel arrangements. We've gone to see Erin a few times and are just now in the process of arranging a family trip to see Angi; to date, I'm the only one who has spent time with her in person. Zack speaks regularly to her on the phone, but both he and his first mother want their relationship to grow. The kids are delighted; so are Judy and I. We now have a way of getting answers to medical and genealogical questions (among others), and most wonderfully, we all care about one another and feel we're members of an extended family. Counterintuitive as it may seem—and true to the research into open adoption—there's no role confusion, divided loyalty, or any of those sorts of concerns. Some parents may have different experiences, but I'm deeply grateful for this transformation in our lives. It might not have happened—and certainly wouldn't have happened as quickly—had I not chosen a different path because of my children.

When I left the *Globe,* I wanted to do everything possible to "normalize" adoption in our culture, so that my kids would no longer have to confront ignorant and often insensitive attitudes. To my mind that meant going beyond advocating for changes targeted specifically at people who were adopted, such as school assignments that imply adoptive families are somehow less legitimate; or media portrayals of adoptees as ingrates or deprived or even (maddeningly) criminals; or laws that strip adopted adults of the same privileges the rest of us receive as a birthright, such as the simple right to obtain our own original birth certificates. If adoption was to become as accepted as any other type of family formation, it was essential to press for better practices and policies, so that the process by which the Zacks and Emmys of the world join their families would become more thoughtful, ethical, and humane not only for the kids but also for both the parents who raise them and the ones who create them.

It wasn't until I conducted the interviews for my *Globe* series that I saw beyond the inaccurate, negative stereotypes of birth mothers. They are not frightened young women who want anonymity, nor are they crass creatures who want to reclaim their children. What a revelation! But that is how our attitudes and laws too often still treat them. My desire to change that reality has become all the stronger as a result of getting to know my own kids' first mothers and hearing directly, from them, how difficult their decisions were and how deeply they desire to retain a connection to the children they bore. They, like nearly all their counterparts, have reinforced the truth I discovered while researching my series and book: virtually no woman can carry a life inside her, feel the child emerge, then pretend it never happened. If there is such a thing as an accurate stereotype, I believe it is that birth mothers care deeply and eternally about the boys and girls they created, but invariably come to terms—for the sake of those children—with the reality that other people have become their parents.

Did I mention that I've developed some strong opinions about adoption?

After about a year of writing, researching, and speaking about adoption—and struggling financially—I was offered my current post at the Evan B. Donaldson Adoption Institute. The stars could not have aligned more perfectly. Now my passion for my children was not only something I would carry with me each day, it would be my job, and one that paid the bills to boot.

So the transformation is complete. Once the detached observer, I am now an emotionally driven and highly motivated advocate for the institution that transformed my life: adoption. I know how sappy that sounds, but it is the path I travel from the time I awake every morning until I retire at night. I admit I talk too much about the issues I care about to friends at dinner, to family members during visits, and

sometimes to people I don't know at neighborhood barbe-
cues. Like I said, it's all adoption, all the time.

And I expect it to remain that way for the foreseeable
future. Though the adoption process has improved in many
ways over the last decade, there's still so much to do to create
a future for our kids in which ill-conceived laws, antiquated
policies, and discriminatory practices cease to undercut them
and their families. We live in a world, after all, in which the
words "you're adopted" are still commonly wielded as an insult or invoked to conjure a distasteful stereotype. While
most reputable journalists have long since banned the practice of identifying news subjects by race, gender, or religion
unless it has direct bearing on the story at hand, the adjec-
tive "adopted" still crops up meaninglessly in account after
account. It is a subtle suggestion that this person is somehow "other," somehow different, somehow problematic.

That observation is neither preachy nor overstated. It is
a statement of unacceptable fact—and, for me, it changes
everything.

Across Two Cultures

EMILY PRAGER

From the moment I brought my daughter home from China, I wanted her to stay connected with her birth land. I remember being on the airplane coming home and fantasizing about having a Chinese babysitter, planning how my child could stay in touch with her language. This was eleven years ago and it was not exactly accepted in adoption circles to feel this way. Actually, other adoptive parents thought I was wacky.

My reasons back then for keeping LuLu's past afloat were simple. Foremost, I wanted her to keep that Chinese language map in her head. I had read a book by a Chinese-American graduate of Harvard that spoke of the loneliness he'd felt at college not being able to speak Chinese, and how this hole in his education had kept him apart from other Chinese students. I didn't want my daughter to grow up adrift between two cultures, unable to communicate with her

Chinese countrymen. Also, it was clear that China was going to be a major player in world markets; I wanted her to have a solid base on which to learn one of the world's most difficult languages.

And I love China. I spent three years of my childhood in Taiwan, and I remain in thrall with the sensibility of this land of water plants and its people. I wanted her to appreciate the place of her birth as much as I did. I had no idea then how important connecting her to her heritage would turn out to be.

A few months after returning home to New York City, I began casting around for a Chinese babysitter. Many phone conversations later, I connected with a network of Chinese women who wanted to supplement their incomes but did not speak English. They were the well-educated wives of men in computer programs at the local university where I was teaching, and their friends. My first babysitter was a doctor from Beijing who was studying to take the licensing exams here. My second was an extraordinary woman named Hu, who'd been a medical researcher in China. A deeply caring woman, she had been through hell during the Cultural Revolution because her father was a doctor. I'll never forget a mother coming up to me on the playground one day and saying, "Your babysitter, she is wonderful. She cares for your child as if she were her own." When Hu's husband got a job in Minneapolis, I cried. But after another round of phone calls, Ling appeared. The wife of a diplomat, she wore big black glasses. She came to work with a ball gown in her bag, which she changed into at the end of the day to attend embassy parties.

I don't know if it made much difference to my baby daughter, but I like to think the presence of these soothing Chinese faces and voices eased her transition from a Chinese orphanage to New York City by providing some familiarity. She seemed very happy with her sitters, and never, as some parents fear, confused them with me.

Around the time my child turned two, I decided to send her to a preschool in Chinatown. I phoned the China Institute and, after obtaining a recommendation, checked out the downtown address. I'll never forget stepping through an unattractive outer door to find Shangri-la within. Beautifully decorated with leaves and fairy trees, and appointed with shiny wood floors and little wooden tables and chairs, the Red Apple Child Development Center was glorious. It was also what I had been hoping for: home-cooked Chinese meals for lunch, music lessons from age three, Mandarin spoken all day long. To top it off, the owner and manager, Mrs. Fan, who had a master's in education from New York University, envisioned building a multicultural school— the best of the East and the West, as she recounted it to me. I enrolled my daughter instantly.

If people thought I was odd hiring Chinese babysitters, they thought I'd lost my mind when I packed LuLu off to Red Apple. In those days, non-Chinese parents didn't head down to Chinatown and drop off their kids. But I felt this was the last opportunity my daughter would have for the rest of her school days to be immersed in Chinese life. In my home, she would live a predominantly non-Chinese existence among mostly non-Chinese people.

I also hoped that through this school LuLu would learn

to take pride in being Chinese. There were, I felt, a lot of things I could teach my daughter: pride in being an American, pride in being a woman, pride in (and respect for) the history of her birth culture. But I think pride in one's race comes from seeing people of your race doing things to be proud of. This, she saw at Red Apple, and I will always love the teachers there for it. I remember, after LuLu had been at the school about a year, taking her to see the Disney film *Mulan*. In the lobby of the theater, my daughter stopped in front of a big poster of Mulan. Beaming, she shouted, "She's Chinese! I'm Chinese, too!" and an incredible smile spread across her face.

What my daughter gained from Red Apple was something precious. During her three years at Red Apple, she learned through the loving Chinese women who taught her to appreciate the strength of her genetics. For my part, I learned what it was like to be in the minority, to be the only member of your race in a room, to have people look at you and wonder what you were doing there and how you got in. As LuLu watched me cope, she saw that I was initially self-conscious and a bit awkward; then she saw me relax with it and no longer feel like the odd woman out.

LuLu was a pioneer, too. No one at the school had ever seen, much less met, an adopted Chinese girl. The teachers and parents had dimly heard about such adoptions maybe. But their notion of what these girls might be like drifted in and out of our conversations. One time when LuLu had been there a few years, a teacher said to me, "She came here as a country girl but now she's a city girl." And she gave me a thumbs-up.

By the time LuLu graduated in 1999, we had all changed. By then, Families with Children from China, a fast-growing network of adoptive families, was sponsoring Chinese classes at the school. Lots of members' children now occupied the chairs at the tiny wooden tables. Just as Mrs. Fan had dreamed, Red Apple, like China, was opening to the West.

In her years at Red Apple, my daughter had been working on understanding her complex identity. We had discussed the difference in our looks, the fact that she had grown in another mother's body, that she had come from China. One day, I decided that before primary school began, my child and I should visit her hometown of Wuhu, a gentle city on the Yangtze River in south central Anhui Province. As we set out, I hoped that the trip would clarify her understanding of her situation.

What I could never have guessed was how beneficial our trip would be. During our three-month stay, LuLu attended preschool, and we lived at a central hotel, which meant that we became known to quite a lot of people. Wuhu was her town, and the townspeople accepted her as if she had never left. My whirling-dervish daughter, known for her energy and busy pace, grew calmer and calmer as the weeks went by. It was as if there had been a space in her heart that she filled with movement, and now it was being filled with the warmth of the people of her town and the beauty of the trees with the magnolia buds as big as footballs.

Often, on walks through the town, LuLu and I spoke of her birth mother. I pointed out the factories where her birth mother might work now, areas in which she might live, and we both, in our own ways, came to a sense of reality about her mother and who she might be. Of course, we did not meet her. LuLu, like most of the girls who wind up in China's orphanages, had been abandoned. But her birth mother became a flesh-and-blood person in our minds, much like the young women we met.

Our days in Wuhu changed my daughter and me. Our visit gave her the ability to really know what it means when she says "I was born in China." And as the people of my daughter's hometown came to accept me as LuLu's mother (interracial adoption was new to them), I realized that Wuhu was a hometown to me, too; that I was now part of her birth family and they were part of mine.

Upon our return to New York City, as LuLu had turned five in China, I began to scout primary schools. If I had been aware of the importance of her heritage before, this search brought the truth of her situation into even sharper focus. As an adoptive parent, I know that I do and I don't see my child as Chinese. Though I am aware of it visually, most days I don't register it consciously at all. But as I went around to the area's private and public schools with enviable reputations, I suddenly realized how white they were. Schools I had wanted for her seemed almost racist to me.

At one school, a very good school I had thought, a sign was posted on the front door that read, ASIAN NIGHT, with a date and time. "Asian Night," I thought dully, as we began the tour. When our guide, himself a parent, told me I would have to join "the minority parents' committee," I knew I would never send my daughter to this school. What kind of message does it send a kindergartner to be pegged as a minority child from the first day of school, regardless of the truth of the statement? Should any child ever be "a minority child"? In my eyes it was—and is—a diminishment. I ended up sending LuLu to an international school. The moment I walked through the front door and saw the diverse mix of children, I knew it was the right place.

Up until the search for schools, I had still thought LuLu's Chineseness didn't really matter in the scheme of things. Seeing the whiteness of those school populations showed me otherwise. It reminded me that I shouldn't be naive or in denial, that to the outer world, my child is Chinese, for better or worse, and that is a fact.

Once again, I was struck with the importance of connecting LuLu with her genetic heritage. I saw the necessity of her knowing and feeling the power of the ten thousand years of history and art and culture that flow through her veins. It was this power base, combined with her family's love, that would get her through any racial problems she might encounter.

And encounter them she did. That first year of kindergarten on the school bus that ferried children from many schools, not just her own, some lout teased her about her eyes and nose, prompting our first talk about racism. Other cruel incidents would follow in the years ahead. The worst, in my opinion, came during a soccer class when she was eight. Two boys, seeing me waiting near the fence, taunted her, saying, "You're adopted, aren't you?"

"Yes," she replied. "Something wrong with that?"

"Yeah," said one. "Your parents didn't love you."

When LuLu told me about this, I remember thinking, "My God, will she have to go through this her whole life?" I was crushed for her. I couldn't believe the cruelty. But I have learned over the years not to program her reactions and color them with my own. So I held myself back. "What did you say to that?" I asked.

"I told them they were wrong, and I explained about China's one-child policy and how women had to give up their daughters," she replied. "And they apologized."

As LuLu gets older and develops more outside interests, it becomes harder and harder, as I feared so long ago, for her to connect with her genetic heritage. That's given me the chance to concentrate on her adoptive heritage, on her great-grandparents and how they came from Ireland and Russia, and settled here, and how everyone got together. I realized I was so bent on connecting her with her birth land that I sort of forgot my own ancestors, taking it for granted that she would absorb their presence. I do a lot more about them now—in fact, life's mostly about them these days. But in every family tree she makes at school, she draws two branches, one for her birth clan, one for us.

Nowadays, LuLu attends folk dance class in Chinatown. She is a natural folk dancer, my daughter. When the girls dress up in traditional Chinese costumes, another adoptive mother and I cry because in some very deep way, that's who our daughters are. We are both so moved by it and so very proud to be associated with them.

When I look back, I'm glad I was such a nut about heritage, because I think when I decided to embrace my child's birth family and land and not be afraid that if she saw them clearly, she would love them more than me, it somehow released her. I think it helped her to begin to embrace herself and her origins. I know it helped her to fully embrace us, her adoptive family. Adoption, our search for heritage taught me, is a two-way street. We intertwine our families and our lives and our ancestors and there never has to be any taking away.

The Orphan Myth

DOUG HOOD

woman sat next to me at a bus station in Nicaragua, patted her swollen belly, and asked, "Do you want this baby?" This was back in the eighties, when I was in my late thirties. The place smelled of a dead animal, and I was feeling scorched. I glanced at her belly but continued to drink my Coke and act as if it were nothing, as if she were offering me her sandals.

I was there with Healing the Children, a nonprofit group of medical misfits, on another stop in a poor country where the children with malformed cleft lips and disfiguring burns streamed in to see us, expecting miracles. I had already been with medical teams in Colombia, Ecuador, and Guatemala and had seen a lot of kids with bleak futures, no homes. But I had never had an offer to take one. After a sleepless night I realized I had an answer to that woman's idle desperation: yes.

I t was a big day, American clinic day, the following year in Santa Ana, El Salvador. The peeling hallways were filled with shoulder-high *campesinos* from all over the country scraping together all they had to bring in their kids with hellacious disfigurations. Near the end of that day one little girl, alone in a plain dress, stood at the door. Although eleven, she was like a lot of kids there, stunted, appearing years younger. She had a massive red-mottled scar flowing like lava from her chin down to her abdomen. Her neck was frozen in flexion to where she had to lean back to merely peer straight ahead. It was all from a kerosene stove. I asked the nurse to get her parents.

"Jefe, no tiene padres." Her parents had dropped her off at the hospital six months earlier, wrapped in wet newspaper, and had never come back. She remained a hospital urchin, the only cost being her daily scoops of rice and beans. "Rosa Alexandra believes you will save her," added the nurse.

Each morning on ward rounds little Rosa shadowed me like I was her dad, being my gofer for supplies. On the day of her surgery I lifted her onto the stretcher and lovingly mussed her black hair before they wheeled her off. In the OR the local anesthesiologist, who looked nineteen, gave her an agent that paralyzed her before he was to intubate her. Because of her severely twisted neck he floundered trying to jam the tube into her throat, causing chaos to erupt. Through the din she lay there unable to breathe. Just like that Rosa Alexandra was dead. They swathed her body in a cloth, and a driver took her back to her parents' house in the mountains.

Another girl, three years younger, had arrived earlier at the clinic, virtually a bookend of Rosa. Her name was Nancy and she had the same burn, the same wrenched neck, and I envisioned the same grisly fate. I told Nancy's orphanage director that she was coming to the United States for her surgery. Registered as a foster parent, I flew Nancy to Connecticut. A hospital took care of the surgery without charge, operating twice to release her neck.

Nancy became a mini-celebrity in the community. For me she was something more—a chance to be a parent. The seed that had been planted in Nicaragua had taken root with Rosa: I wanted to adopt an orphan. But the three months with this foster child caused me to rethink. Despite the community's outpouring of warmth, Nancy remained stony and cold. After her recuperation, with teary-eyed friends, I put Nancy, with her new neck and a dozen boxes of toys and clothes, on a flight home. As we parted, I felt spent, and as though I were hugging a mannequin.

Despite the self-doubt, my dream was to adopt an orphan, and it wouldn't go away. Word had it that a single man could not adopt. Then came news about China relaxing its policies. I phoned an agency in Seattle and they said, "We've never done it but we can try." One year later, I was standing in Hangzhou when a creaky door opened and there stood my scared four-and-a-half-year-old Suki.

That was nine years ago. Suki revived me from a late-forties life of spiraling ennui and athletic nostalgia. Dramatic sacrifices I was warned about never happened. Instead of giving up the things I loved, I combined them—Suki learned to sweat and grunt along with me. You'd see me pulling or pushing her on my marathons, swims, and bike rides. Before long my once bowlegged Suki was ripped, muscling alongside me stride for stride.

She also teamed with me in becoming a denizen of the world's back alleys and high plateaus. Suki stuffed our satchels and mastered the trickery of long-term parking and the spaghetti waiting lines at JFK, where we headed off for unpronounceable destinations. Without maps, itineraries, or reservations, we crossed Mongolia in a jeep, hopped by jungle plane to Panama's San Blas Islands, traversed Lake Titicaca to Bolivia in a fishing boat, and took a taxi through the barrios of Cuba.

The lesson I drilled was the taxi driver will teach us more than the museum, even if he charges us double at the end.

Our trips were at times edgy, as when we crossed a small windy sea in an Indian canoe, and at times isolating, like when we were cooped up for two days in a Reykjavik ice storm. But missing from them were the life-altering hangovers I had with Healing the Children. HTC had a strict policy about its teams: no children allowed. I'd resigned myself to sitting out the years, as if on probation, until Suki reached the magical age of sixteen.

One year, with funding from Gillette, HTC was desperate to set up sites in several Chinese cities. My three trips to China with Suki qualified me, by default, as an expert, and they called. I said I'd go, but only one way: with my precious nine-year-old. Part of our charm, I guess, was our predicament. Suki would have to go everywhere with me, sometimes with a friendly blind eye, from men's rooms to emergency rooms to boardrooms. HTC came back with an okay.

As we prepared for the trip I told Suki what she'd see: glimpses of her life-what-could-have-been, including some orphans, people speaking to her in Chinese, and kids with split lips. My path, with her in tow, had included many late-night on-call runs to the ER, where Suki once helped look for a missing finger, and we've been back to her orphanage, where, over a free dumpling lunch, the director was tight-lipped about Suki's first years. With all that behind her, Suki looked at me dismissively and said, "Daddy, enough chitchat. I'll be okay." It's about as much dialogue as I ever squeeze out of her.

Suki and I started out in the west in Kunming, where we scalded our tongues with their famous hot pots, worked our way across the breadth of China to Shenyang in the north, and then snaked south to Shanghai and Beijing. As we shared *maotai* at the dinner table with the president of Yunnan University and the next week with the leader of Shanghai, the center of our conversations wasn't the site approvals, it was Suki. Gentlemen, let me explain: this little ambassador you can't take your eyes off was once a Hangzhou orphan bound for oblivion.

After those sites were approved, Suki and I showed up for duty at the Ninth People's Hospital in Shanghai. While I worked the recovery room, Suki spent most of her days at the nurses' station stapling papers. One day the nurses coaxed a strong-armed Suki over to help move one of the Chinese orphans, a bulky post-op who had undergone massive reconstructive surgery. Her name was Zhang Su Xin. Like a mummy, she was bound from the waist up in thick bandages, left only with holes for her arms, nose, and mouth. Suki was drawn in by the girl with no face.

When Su Xin's hand blindly reached out for Suki, she clutched it and stayed. Suki asked me, Can you find her eyes? I led her fingers to the impressions in the bandages. An interpreter arrived and the girls traded stories. At the age of ten Su Xin had had lice in her hair and the orphanage aides had soaked it with gasoline. She had leaned too close to a stove and been engulfed in flames.

Each day Suki returned to Su Xin's bedside, helping to spoon-feed and bathe her. Su Xin, with her free hands, relied on some gestures, from which she and Suki created a language of signals, bonding through their fingertips. Suki showed Su Xin origami; they made baby swans and peanut-sized stars. By her bed were pictures of her before and after the accident. Once, she stood next to a small waterfall, her smiling face like porcelain. And then the very same girl looked like a waxy creation for a Hollywood thriller.

The incineration did nothing to diminish hope in Su Xin. She said she wanted to be a musician, so a guitar was found. Our last day she gave Suki her only stuffed toy, a furry tree trunk with three little squirrels. Eventually, she would return to her orphanage. Suki asked, "Daddy, what will happen then?" I told her Su Xin would become a great musician. My answer was hollow and I sensed Suki knew it. I saw a rare pensive moment in her, maybe my same feeling of helplessness.

One quiet evening after we returned to Connecticut, I asked Suki if she would like to do more work for orphans like Su Xin. She could build on it, like a project, I added.

"A project?"

"I mean instead of just going to places and finding silly *milagros* toys like we did in Mexico, we look up orphanages."

"And do what?"

"You know, help them. Maybe you could write about it for school. See if it leads to something."

"I have to write about it?" Immediately I wanted to backtrack. She asked, "Did you have a project when you were a kid?"

"Me? Nothing like that." I said, "Suki, I want you to find some focus and this is perfect. It fits what we do. Don't be like me and wait till you're forty."

Perhaps, at first, it sounded like a gargantuan term paper. Suki is a doer, not a reader, not a planner, not a writer. I regret those *not* parts, but wouldn't change anything. There's something nonsensical but magical, I can't describe it, in what she does. She'd sooner build a brick wall as write two pages about it. In our little family I am the idea-spinning Don Quixote she's always poking fun at, and she's the one that fixes the squeaky bike.

"Look, Suki," I said, "I'll get you there."

"Okay, and I'll do stuff like with Su Xin."

After a little research on orphans, Suki said, "Everywhere you look, there's millions. Doesn't anyone pay attention?"

I said, "There's a myth about them."

"What do you mean, Daddy?"

"People almost think they don't exist."

Our next trip, the following winter, was to Chile via Honduras.

At the Parque Central in Tegucigalpa we asked about any nearby orphanages and were led to an address three blocks away. I pressed a buzzer beside a solid door with a sign overhead, El Hogar de Esperanza, whispering to Suki, "House of Hope." Someone peered through a hole but the door opened immediately when I said the word "Americans." We introduced ourselves to the director, a handsome Honduran, asking if we could look around. He took us right to the courtyard, where some fifty kids scurried around. Suki timidly kicked the soccer ball with them. Many were curious about our odd pairing. The girls were shy and needed coaxing but the boys swarmed us and threw their arms for attention.

The director told us most come off the street, assigned by the government. He emphasized they all felt lucky to be there. He showed me the various rooms, and finally in the last one we noticed a woman in a Red Sox T-shirt with light hair that fell loose, partly hiding her face. Upon hearing my voice, she stopped what she was doing and gasped, "Finally, I can speak English."

Over lunch, the striking woman, Julie, from Maine, explained how she initially used vacation time from her pediatric practice in Boston to look at the glue addiction among the street kids, but eventually got "a little obsessed," finally selling her practice. She cursed a Wisconsin shoe glue company that she said knowingly pockets most of their revenue from the addicted kids. "The kids get high sniffing it, rob, and, like junkies, pay the stores or shoe guys for more. It does something to their brain. That's what I'm working on," she explained. Julie turned her good career into a better cause, with work that she hoped wouldn't get buried. Teasing Suki, she said, "She's gorgeous. This scares me. I'm afraid I'll take a few home with me."

When we left the restaurant Julie pointed to some of the kids, and said, "The name for them, too bad, is *los gamines*. Seven out of ten are hooked." Some stuck near us like lost pets, and were aggressive with their begging, tapping at our elbows, even slipping fingers into our pockets. They danced and pointed at Suki's eyes.

Later, as Suki and I wandered some city streets, we couldn't help tracking more kids. I spotted a shoe repairman on the street, who unabashedly showed us his glue and even the plastic bags.

One girl always waited by our hotel door day and night. She wore a tattered frilly dress, her bare feet dust-colored and flattened. The hotel doorman waved his finger at us not to give her anything. She'd follow us into a store where the owner would swat and yell at her as if she were a stray dog. Her eyes had a plasticlike sheen, what Julie said was a sign of addiction. At one intersection we saw a shiny-ribbed boy and a rabid-looking dog tugging-war over half a chicken carcass. Suki asked me, "What happens to these kids? Where do they sleep?" I told her their only hope might be House of Hope.

From Tegucigalpa we took a bus toward La Ceiba and to the Caribbean to relax. Even in the white-sand-and-palm setting, we couldn't rid our minds of the homeless kids.

In Chile our plane landed in Santiago. As we walked through the city, I remarked how the men were all the same size, about five-five. There was one popular strip with all shops, mostly music and clothes, not much that interested us. The next day we had a quick flight to Temuco. Up at four the next morning, we took a bus to Puerto Montt and then another to Patagonia, the last stop in the Americas. The bus ride seemed longer because a man with a sagging liver and jaundiced skin kept stumbling down the aisle to use the bathroom unfortunately next to us. Inside he emitted sounds and waves of odor. He'd let the door fly open and other men angrily slammed it, only to hear it unlatch and see it fly open again. Suki'd jab me and my stomach would churn every time she spied him weaving toward us.

Suki and I found a cheap place and planned for our umpteenth Christmas in a strange place, this time in Punta Arenas. Celebration was far from garish, as in our country. For Suki, who has never uttered she wanted anything, I had tucked away some gifts: stuff to make jewelry, a pass for three to the Shubert Theatre, and a picture of a sewing machine waiting back home. We spent Christmas morning sitting at the Strait of Magellan, where across in the swirling mist we could gaze at Tierra del Fuego. This was the height of summer and yet it was windy, drizzly, and cool. We befriended a cab driver, who took us to the German part of town, out to a peninsula to watch the penguins and puffins, then to his own house where we picked up his three daughters. We all had lunch at a small café.

Suki asked him if he knew any orphanages. The driver asked the waitress and then packed us into his cab. When we arrived at the stately brick building, he went up to the door, chatted with someone, then waved us up. We were greeted by two nuns with clasped hands and crisp habits. The first thing that impressed us was a large glass display case of a relief of Patagonia, icebergs and all, made by their kids. Everything was immaculate, the kitchen without a speck, the bedrooms almost military in neatness. The dining room had miniature chairs, and the bathrooms had cups with toothbrushes, each with a name, Enrique, Maria, and so forth. The classroom had a long skinny map of Chile and drawings of Don Quixote and Sancho Panza.

Sister Ana, a woman of regal stature, asked us, as though she was holding back her *pièce de résistance*, "Would you like to meet the children?" She took us to the playground, where the kids were zipping around or milling in small groups. They ranged in age from about four to thirteen. Several circled us with curious stares, their manner natural, playful, and engaging. Some were affectionate with one another, their behavior striking me as the best you (rarely) see in siblings. Drawing closer, they hugged each other tighter, like security blankets. I spotted a budding Pelé, a beauty with Natalie Wood eyes, another called Cheena with eyes like Suki's. One clutched her worn teddy and one girl had a scarf artfully twirled around her neck as if she were strolling on the Champs-Elysée. There was a flirt, a shy one, a boy with bravado pushing a ball into my hand. Linking hands with one giggling girl, Suki joined in the basketball game. They ran herky-jerky in unison, crying in their different languages.

I stood with Sister Ana as she pointed out a few and told me their stories, mostly with parents deceased or disappeared. When I asked if any of the kids could be adopted, she froze momentarily. She turned and responded, "Yes, of course. *Todo.*"

I commented that they looked so happy here, with a communal richness I'd never seen before; it almost seemed a sin to take them away.

She calmly replied, "Everybody's happy when they find a home."

She asked about Suki and I told her our story. Suki's orphanage had had one room with two or three broken toys. She could barely hear, didn't speak a word, four years a blank. The sister asked, "And without you, where would she be?" I answered honestly and said I never think about it.

As I gazed at the kids with the sister's question in mind, my pulse went up. What happens to these kids and others like them everywhere? Kids whose only advocate is Sister Ana? When one child stood close and slipped his hand into mine, his eyes saturated with innocence, I told the sister, "You do a wonderful job here."

She smiled, a subtle smile steeped in the satisfaction of her own long Punta Arenas history, one that with her seventy-year-old eyes told me she is running out of time.

"You're a Chilean treasure." I handed Sister Ana an envelope and shaking my head said, "This is such a weak gesture. I should do more."

She nodded toward Suki, who was surrounded by a dozen kids and struggling but laughing with her Spanish words, and said, "*Señor,* you have."

Special Needs

JENIFER LEVIN

ere you one of the cool kids when you were my age? Van asks.

Remembering thirteen, I wince. *Uh-uh*, I tell him, *not at all.*

The rest of the truth I don't tell him—which is that, at his age, I was such a miserably unpopular scapegoat that I was literally stoned.

Yeah, an ex-lover said once, So what? We were *all* stoned back then.

No, I told her, I was literally *stoned*—I mean in the *biblical* sense of the word. Other kids threw rocks at me when I was walking home from school.

Why? I think I know now. I was a working-class kid in a wealthy town: a stocky, strong, androgynous girl with ugly glasses, shy demeanor, homemade haircut, and uncool clothes—I didn't fit the cheerleader mold, no, not at all.

Adolescents use the appearance of difference and otherness in order to define themselves, and during those years, I fell into the category of other. I moved in the twilit world of the adolescent outcast—a kind of social no-man's-land populated by those who, like me, lacked sufficient status and were considered perfect targets for spitballs, whispered taunts, rubber-band missiles. Our parents and teachers didn't know it—at least, they never knew the extent of it. But those of us who lived through it suffered years of psychological torture at the hands of our peers. It permanently marked us, resulting in a kind of posttraumatic stress syndrome. Socially, this manifested as mistrust, depression, and lack of self-esteem. Some of us recovered and healed. Others didn't.

Feeling unwanted is a terrible and deforming thing, especially for a child. Beneath the suffering and despair, a kind of rage develops. This plays out partly as a desire to get even; to prove to all those tormenters that you're at *least* as desirable as they are. Many a career has been launched on the fuel of such rage. Success brings with it a brutal satisfaction. But as you evolve spiritually, the focus changes. Anger just isn't enough. Inviting love into your life is the real challenge, after all, and abandoning fear of humankind is the precondition. As we grow older, the point becomes to direct rage toward the correct target—injustice of all sorts— then to develop, along with that, compassion for everyone who suffers, and a desire to help when you can.

Over time, I came to understand that surviving as a social and economic outcast in a spoiled-brat community taught me some very useful skills. I learned to hold my own counsel. Learned that pain doesn't necessarily kill. That being unpopular sucks, but not if you understand the flip side, which has to do with being different, even unique; because in a deadeningly homogenized world, difference and uniqueness are *good*. That seeing life through the eyes of an outsider gave me a real wide-angle point of view, allowing me to notice things that eluded others. So it wasn't such a big deal, later on, to go my own way as an artist, or come out of the closet. And when I decided to become a parent in my thirties, the lessons of my suffering adolescence led me to adopt children who faced extra challenges. I swore I'd fight for them, in a way no one had known to fight for me. I'd make sure my children had every opportunity to be fully privileged citizens of the world. They would know they were loved and wanted. I'd focus all of my parental rage and compassion into a protective shield for them, I told myself—until they were grown and could advocate for themselves. I was predisposed emotionally and psychologically to love kids with special needs.

I was right. And wrong. Yes, I knew a lot about being and growing up different. But it didn't exactly prepare me for parenthood. Nothing really does.

My sons, Makara and Vannarith—Mak and Van—are from Cambodia. Both were abandoned to the same Phnom Penh orphanage in the same year—1990—each at the age of a few months. Three years later, my then-girlfriend and I met them there. I stayed in Cambodia and adopted

Mak. Two years after that, she returned to adopt Van. She is now my ex, and we live three blocks apart. The boys live with me a majority of the time, but my ex and I are both dedicated moms and work hard together for them. (How we arrived at this state of friendship and détente is another story.) Our boys aren't biologically related but have known each other longer than they've known anyone else in the world. Both are fourteen-going-on-fifteen. They're handsome and bright: gifted artists, good athletes. And both have numerous special needs, some of which were apparent when we met them, some of which were not. Between the two of them these include a cleft palate, nutritional rickets, asthma, hyperactivity, blood disorders, and multiple learning disabilities. Their needs have required many interventions over the years: surgery, occupational and speech therapy, medication, special schooling.

Reality's not virtual. And adopting children, even when it's extremely difficult, is a lot easier than *raising* children. No book, no expert can prepare you for the twists and turns. Throw special needs into the mix. Shake. Stir. You'll find yourself in another country. Though Van now happily attends a middle school where he makes honor roll and stars in basketball, and Mak promises to be a standout at prep school this year, we move through hard territory and we know it. Keeping it all in perspective is challenging at times; living it, more so.

Yet, against multiple odds, my boys are succeeding. What follows are bits and pieces constituting the unlikely story of their success. It's also the unlikely story of how I—a demon-ridden and impractical artist who, admittedly, didn't know her brain from her behind when it came to raising kids—learned to be their mom.

1994. Mak has been here in the United States for a few months. The speech therapist at a world-renowned hospital is staring at me in shock, because I've just called her stupid. I did so in response to her statement that he would never speak intelligibly. He will always suffer from considerable developmental and language delays, she states with assured expertise, and I should not expect too much. The walls around us are an institutional beige, the linguistic measuring equipment glints. *Gee*, I say, *that's just plain stupid. He will speak beautifully one day.* Much *more beautifully than you.* Realizing, as I say this, that I'm railing against all my own childhood demons, too, and against anyone who belies their demise.

Some months later, after his second craniofacial surgery, he and I build Lego airplanes and hangars one night while *Casablanca* plays on TV in the background. *Casablanca* is sacred in my life. There's nothing like Bogart's tortured face in black-and-white to show you what being a movie star is all about. The multiple layers of affection that are touched upon—passionate eros, loyalty, friendship, partnership, agape—encompass much of love's spectrum. Mak and I put the finishing touches on our cheerfully winged vehicle of multicolored plastic bricks. Out of the corner of my eye I glimpse Rick, smoldering with the bitterness of desire betrayed. A while later I hear him, transformed by an elevated vision of love in the smoky Moroccan night, saying good-bye to Ilsa forever. Telling her what he'd learned from loving her: that the problems of three little people don't amount to a hill of beans in this crazy world. Then speaking those inimitable words full of memory, love, loss, and transcendence: We'll always have Paris.

Arri! Mak chirps, beaming. *Auway ha' Arri!* And while I listen in amazement:

Whew AUWAY ha' ARRI!

Yes! I cry, *That's right, Mak: Paris! Paris!*

ARRI! ARRI!

The preschool admissions committee is having what they call an open and frank discussion—a controversy, really—about accepting Mak, who turns four in the autumn. The issue seems to be whether the school can provide what he needs without diverting resources from the other children—most of whom are white, none of whom have recognizable disabilities. In other words, is he too foreign, too disabled, too different to function in a normal setting? *But he's a regular four-year-old,* the head teacher volunteers. *The kids understand what he says, even when we do not.* I want to bless her, and silently do so. It's true. He's speaking now—unintelligibly to most—but I can make out more and more words over time, and children often respond to his babblings with almost complete comprehension.

Yeah, let's play that.

No, Mak, I can't right now.

Mak, do you want some soup?

Can you say "soup," Mak? Can you say "soup"?

More than a year passes. In a yellow, orange, and black-top city playground sheltered by trees, my boy plays enthusiastically with other five-year-olds. The aluminum slide flashes reflections of sunlight. Colorful, oversized, lightweight balls bounce around. In the two years since Cambodia, Mak has had several operations, thrived at preschool, made lots of little friends, and grown many inches, and he speaks so much more clearly. I watch with happy pride. He's defied the odds.

Suddenly, his smile disappears. His head hangs in a kind of shame. Coming closer, I see why: an older boy and girl, strangers to the group, have joined in and are making fun of his facial scarring, remnants of the surgically corrected cleft that still flattens one side of his nose, still pulls the upper lip ever so faintly into a snarl. I want to make it okay, and approach these young tormenters as I usually do when such situations arise. *Hi. I'm Mak's mom. This is Mak. What are your names?* But instead of being disarmed, these kids just laugh cruelly. *He's a rabbit face! You're not his mom, you're white, you don't even look like him—nobody does.* They race away, damage done, and I'm left holding my wounded son, helpless to protect him, wanting to blow their little blond heads off.

Our scars inform us and, at least in part, define us. The scars my boys carry on their bodies speak to me of unknown origins in a faraway, grieving place that smells of cooked rice, wood smoke, burning sun and relentless rain, dust, human blood, lemongrass. Sitting at my parents' kitchen table with Van one day, soon after his arrival in this country, I hear something familiar and realize that the TV's on in the family room; *Casablanca* is playing. I smile at him quietly; he grins back with a black-toothed, rotting display—a dental appointment is imminent, but during five years of orphanage life his mouth has been heretofore untended. Between that grin and Bogart's televised mutterings, it occurs to me that something important is being said.

"Van, listen to me. *Here's looking at* you, *kid!*"

"Eers ookeen ut *oooo*, ked!"

"Good. Fantastic. Again: *Here's looking at* you, *kid!*"

"Eers ookeen ut *oooo*, ked!"

Remember, I tell him, remember those words. And say them, someday, to your own true love. God knows we couldn't afford even one kid, much less two. But I knew we were in trouble—a good kind of trouble—the minute I saw you standing near the orphanage gates with your crooked little legs. And I said to myself, *Of all the gin joints in the world, why'd he have to show up in mine?*

Van's fingers, wrists, and calves, twisted by childhood rickets, are growing straighter and stronger. Here for some months now, he is picking up English quickly. Aside from Mak, though, he hasn't yet made friends. It is my great hope (the hope of any parent, really) that he will soon. But in the playground one day, some kids decide on a game with brutal rules: he will be a monster named Crooked Man;

they will be the good guys running away. When I approach, he is sobbing. *I not monster! I good guy!* That's right, I tell him, trying to soothe. I turn to the others, desperate to give him a chance at enfranchisement. Van's not the monster, I tell them firmly, I am. This one time, it works: he grins immediately, and all of them run from me, giggling, as I chase them around the monkey bars. Later on, though, he is deserted again. I watch him suddenly climb the long, long pole supporting a swing set. He perches at the top making shrill, lonely sounds. *Vanny!* I call. And in Khmer, *Vannarith! Ta-ow nee chia-muy mai!* Come here to Mom. But he doesn't seem to hear. I am desolate.

Later, struggling with my terrible Khmer and his smatterings of English, I manage to ask what it was that he felt. With the poetry of fresh, barely formed language, he holds a hand to his nose and sniffs, animal-like. *No feel. I smell.*

Okay, I ask then, *what does it smell like?*

It smell like fire scrape my heart.

In the pediatric craniofacial wards of major hospitals, you see faces literally torn apart and rebuilt. Your anguish is considerable when one of the faces belongs to your very own child. But for all of the reconstructive surgeries Mak undergoes to correct congenital deficiencies of lip and palate, throat, nose, and inner ears (to prevent loss of hearing, common with his condition), there are so many kids in worse shape. Kids with an eye where their chin's supposed to be, a nose instead of an ear, half a mouth, no forehead.

Sometimes he comes out of the anesthesia crying in pain, then looks over at one of these kids in the next bed and is suddenly silent. You can almost hear him thinking, "Oh, *man!*" It gives him a kind of patience, I think, supports his very young sense of dignity. Over the years, the quiet dignity and patience with which he accepts his ordeals have a calming effect on me. If he can deal, so can I.

There are lighthearted times, too. Praise from art and cartooning teachers. Mak paints a self-portrait—smiling, wide-eyed, scar and all—that is astonishingly sophisticated, and everyone says how good it is. Van's limbs grow stronger and straighter; he proves possessed of extraordinary coordination and of a sure, wiry strength. He's an instant success in Little League, Rookie of the Year at age nine and named to an All-Stars team. Mak's path is less glorious: He rides the bench for three seasons; then, after years of occupational therapy and batting cage practice, breaks out in his fourth season to smash homer after homer over the fence.

Despite all their work and these moments of much-celebrated success, at school my boys make friends but do not thrive. Sometimes, they are cruelly teased. Academically, they fall behind. I don't know whether or not this breaks their hearts, but it sure breaks mine. Van's athletic prowess ensures his status on the playing field. Yet he is failing in other areas, and it's chipping away at the core of him. He's always been a fighter—fighting for affection, then fighting against it. Now, though, he's clearly miserable, socially inadequate, and losing the will to fight for good things. I become hated by the special education committee in our public school district. They obviously dread the sound of my voice, and I am increasingly impatient with the time it takes to get even insufficient services in place for my boys. It's lawyer time. Battling Van (who hates change) and the system all the way, I get him into a private school for bright children with learning disabilities. My ex and I sue the district to help foot the bill for private school. After many months, they capitulate, and settle.

For Mak—despite occasional triumphs like artwork and home runs—the road also grows harder and the way unclear. Tall for his age, gangly, with residual clumsiness even after years of occupational therapy, he enters preadolescence with head hanging low and shoulders stooped, grows his hair shaggy, wary of looking others in the eye. The adults in his life have long since ceased to see the tiny scar between his lip and nose; we've stopped noticing his underbite, which gives the impression of an enlarged jaw—really, as is typical with his condition, the result of an underdeveloped ("insufficient") palate—and pushes his upper teeth askew, deforming the speech he has so worked to attain. But with kids, difference is everything. Gazing at him, we see our handsome, gentle son. Gazing at himself in a mirror, all he sees is a scar. He is bright, intuitive, with a charming sense of humor. Yet his struggles with speech and hearing translate into perceptual and cognitive difficulties, and my bright, charming boy falls behind many of his classmates. He begins to call himself stupid.

I look to middle school, where awareness of difference becomes so much more acute, where acceptance by peers is everything. I fear that he will become a scapegoat—at best a class clown. I fear that he will become as I was. And deter-

mine not to let that happen. As with Van before him, my ex
and I face a district board of education that refuses to admit
its own failure. Supported by years of professional evalua-
tion, specialized testing, and bureaucratic paperwork, we
win a private school placement for him and again sue the
district. After another year of hostility and red tape, we win.

Mak's resistance to the change is not as fierce as Van's.
But in a quieter way it is there nonetheless. "I ain't gonna go
to no damn special school!"

"'I'm *not* gonna go to *any* damn special school.' And you
are gonna go."

"*No!* Why do I gotta go to some damn—"

"Because you're smart, and you deserve to be in a school
where people really understand how to teach you."

"Ha-ha! Now *he* gotta go *too!*" Van grins.

"Oh," I sigh, exasperated. "Did I ask for *your* opinion, dude?"

Winter 2003. After years of struggle, many of them
spent in doctors' visits, paperwork, litigation, expensive applications, and professional evaluations (during which
time I worked two jobs, and my ex plenty of overtime), Van
is ensconced in his little school and succeeding academically
for the first time in his life. Mak is accepted at another
school, and about to begin having genuine success. So I decide to undergo some necessary surgery that I've been
putting off for months. And almost die.

Following a straightforward operation, I suffer complica-
tions and insist on being discharged too soon. A few days

later I am rushed back in an ambulance through the snow-storm of the year. The sounds of tire chains on snow mingle with the voices of paramedics trying to keep me awake, and death shimmers around the edges of my consciousness—for the first time ever, a distinct possibility. Feeling it, I am surprised. I'd always expected that it would manifest as fear and struggle and clinging to life; and, too, I'd expected to see some sort of otherworldly light. What I experience instead is a dull and distant apathy; what I see is a gentle graying of things. I worry, in a vaguely detached way: What if the Buddhists are wrong, and there is no reincarnation? Then I think: *Fuck it.* And, in a moment, I completely understand the real physical nature of life's diminishment and eventual loss.

What I cling to in the end, through wretched illness and pain, is the thought of my two young sons. And of how, if I do not care about staying alive for myself, I must at least stay alive to be with them. So I do the practical thing, and fight in my own unglamorous way for life. This time around, I win.

Mak is relatively unflappable throughout. "I been through lots of surgery," he says simply, during a visit. "It's no big deal."

Van is less composed. "Awww," he cries, with a hint of that old desolate shriek from the top of a playground swing set, "I just want things to get *normal!*"

Looking back, I will realize how funny it is, really: This troubled boy with gorgeous visage, multiple talents, and differences galore, yearning for the abnormal normality of a queer mom and extended family and doctors and therapists and special needs schools. But there it is—his panicked yearning for some imaginary state of perfection, afforded by my imperfect presence in his life—and it forces me into a practical frame of mind.

Hospitalized for more than two months, I have plenty of time to contemplate difficult truths. Plenty of time to understand how deeply the roots of my own existence intertwine with the lives of my sons. To finally know once and for all that the pain and shame of my own adolescent past is finished and must not shadow or deform their hopeful young lives. I take serious stock of myself. I am not rich or at ease, and I cannot always protect the people I love—although, goodness knows, I try. I do not have the life I dreamed of in my own tortured youth. But in a totally unexpected way, I have just the life that I need. I never achieved revenge; I achieved something better instead. And it isn't I who saved the lives of my sons; it is they who, unsuspecting, saved mine.

Lying there full of tubes and drugs, I say good-bye to whatever childhood demons still stand between me and love. Scars shape all of us, but need not twist us out of shape.

Months later: Summer. The Sunken Forest on Fire Island where, for the first time since the hospital, I will run with my long-legged son. *Go on,* I tell him, *you're a lot faster, Mak. When we get to the forest, though, wait for me.* Between ocean breeze and the smell of wood, through wild dunes and astonishingly thick green shrubbery, I plod along slowly, painfully, watching him race far ahead. At the crest of a hill he turns, trotting easily back to me with a slightly bewildered grin.

How come you're so slow now, Mai?

Well, because I was sick from the surgery. It's taking a long time to get better.

So? It never took me this long.

That is true.

Ah, I say, and smile. *You are so much younger.*

He accepts this with a shrug. And lopes on. I am touched by it: this kid who's seen me lift weights, run strongly, swim quickly, accepts a more aged and limited me with humor, without hesitation. And it's perfect in a way, the two of us running—one very slow now, one so graceful and fast—he, for whom I used to wait open-armed at the tops of stairs and at street corners as he fought to catch up, now patiently waiting for me.

Later, on a wind-streaked beach, I tell him we must take our shoes off. Why? he asks. Oh, I say, to jump into the water.

"With our clothes on?"

I nod.

He giggles, momentarily a very young child again. But we untie our training flats and strip off socks, and I can feel fresh sand between toes, sand that is hot, then coolly damp, and the chill, salty shock of the water. I gasp, then turn to see him hesitate at that frothy line where sea meets land. Come on, son! I urge. We're laughing.

Last breath of his childhood, I think, *last gasp of my youth.*

But that's as it should be. I suppose you could say that in my adolescence I learned shame; in my adulthood, strength; in my parenthood, humility.

My son moves ahead, hesitates again for a moment in that state between childhood and manhood, then plunges forward, immersing himself. We ride waves. We splash, fully clothed, in the water.

A year later, late summer. Things are normal. Well, as normal as they get. The boys are shooting hoops with friends in the playground.

I always wanted ease, and perfection. At least, that's what I *think* I wanted. But truth be told, what I *needed* was the difficulty. *Im*perfection. What I needed was the struggle.

I tell myself:

Welcome to Casablanca.

Oh, I know. This isn't where you thought you'd wind up. You were made for more perfect destinations. Yet here you are instead, in Casablanca: a crucible of peril, imperfection, transformation. Where everyone has special needs.

But listen: I will tell you a secret. Here, in Casablanca, you can get just what you need and just what you truly yearn for— if you are willing to pay the price. Then, too, you may be blessed with a modicum of grace. And love without rage. And memory without bitterness. For there is love, there is grace, in the world.

I tell my sons: Casablanca is a state of mind. An intermediate place of turbulence, of suffering and transcendence, as passion flares, then ebbs, and wisdom grows. Call it life.

I tell them: There is another place, too, where perfection dwells. You once were there, if only in your heart. It lives, glowing, inside you. The point is not to attain it, but to reach for it. To remember it. Call it paradise. Call it Paris.

I tell them: Here's looking at you, kids.

ACKNOWLEDGMENTS

Our thanks to Susan Caughman, Dottie Enrico, Christina Frank, Christina Baker Kline, and Jacqueline Mitchard for their assistance in getting this project launched; Josh Lerman for introducing us to some of the writers in this collection; our editor, Megan Lynch, for her enthusiasm and formidable diplomacy skills; our agent, Gail Hochman, for her unflagging support from start to finish; our husbands, David Rosenzweig and Joe Treen, for their ideas and support; our daughters, Emily, Annie, and Becky, for their encouragement and patience; and our wonderful contributors for digging deep to share their stories with us.

ABOUT THE CONTRIBUTORS

MARCELLE CLEMENTS is the author of two novels, *Midsummer* and *Rock Me*. She also wrote the nonfiction book *The Improvised Woman: Single Women Reinventing Single Life,* and *The Dog Is Us,* a collection of essays. Her articles and essays on culture, politics and the arts have appeared in many national publications. She also teaches at New York University. Clements lives in New York City with her son, Luc, ten, who was born in San Antonio.

LAURA SHAINE CUNNINGHAM is the author of nine books, including the acclaimed memoirs *Sleeping Arrangements* and *A Place in the Country,* the novels *Beautiful Bodies* and *Dreams of Rescue,* and the young adult novel of an adopted Russian girl, *The Midnight Diary of Zoya Blume.* Her work has been excerpted in *The New Yorker* and the *New York Times.* She lives in New York with her daughters Alexandra, fourteen, who was born in Romania, and Jasmine, twelve, who was born in China.

CHRISTINA FRANK is a writer specializing in health, psychology, relationships, and parenting. Her articles have appeared in many national magazines, including *Health, Redbook, Glamour, Biography, Parenting,* and *Harper's Bazaar.* She and her husband, Josh Lerman, live in Brooklyn, New York, with their two daughters. Their oldest, Olivia, nine, is biological; Lucy, four, was adopted from Vietnam at six months.

About the Contributors

JESSE GREEN is the author of the adoption memoir *The Velveteen Father: An Unexpected Journey to Parenthood,* which received a Lambda Literary Prize and was named to several of 1999's best-book lists. He is an award-winning journalist and regular contributor to the *New York Times* Arts & Leisure section, and his articles have appeared in *The New Yorker,* the *New York Times Magazine,* the *Washington Post, New York, Premiere, Philadelphia, GQ, Out, Elle, O, Rosie,* and *7 Days.* His works of fiction include the novel *O Beautiful,* and short stories that have appeared in *Mademoiselle, Mississippi Review,* and *The American Voice.* Green lives in Brooklyn, New York, with his partner, Andy, and their two sons, Erez, eleven, and Lucas, nine, who were adopted at birth in a Southwestern state.

MELISSA FAY GREENE is the author of *Praying for Sheetrock* and *The Temple Bombing* (both National Book Award finalists), and 2003's *Last Man Out: The Story of the Springhill Mine Disaster.* Greene has been a regular contributor to *The New Yorker, The New York Times Magazine, Life, Good Housekeeping, Reader's Digest,* and the *Washington Post.* She and her husband, Don Samuel, live in Atlanta. Their seven children are Molly, twenty-three, Seth, twenty, Lee, seventeen, Lily, thirteen, Fisseha, eleven, Jesse, ten, and Helen, nine. Jesse arrived from Bulgaria in 1999, Helen from Ethiopia in 1996, and Fisseha from Ethiopia in 2004. Melissa's latest book is about a foster mother to AIDS orphans in Addis Ababa, Ethiopia.

DOUG HOOD's short stories have appeared in *Cimarron Review, Northeast Corridor,* and other literary magazines. His essays about adoption have been published in *The Advocate, Adoptive Families,* and *Adoption Today,* and anthologized in *A Passage to the Heart: Writings from Families with Children from China.* He also is the author of a children's book, *The Stone Hat.* A single father, Hood lives in Connecticut with his daughter, Suki, who was adopted from China at age four. Now fourteen, Suki received a Healing the Children award for her help with Chinese orphans.

PAMELA KRUGER is a writer and editor, specializing in women, work, and family issues. Her articles have appeared in the *New York Times, Fast Company, Parenting, Redbook, Good Housekeeping, The International Herald Tribune,* and others. She's been a contributing editor at *Fast Company,* a contributor to the *New York Times,* and an editorial consultant to Time Inc. and Lifetime Television's website. Currently a contributing editor at *Child* magazine, she is also an adjunct journalism professor at New York University. She and her husband, David Rosenzweig, live in New Jersey, with their two daughters. Emily, nine, is biological, and Annie, four, was adopted from Kazakhstan at six months.

JENIFER LEVIN is the author of the novels *Water Dancer* (Pen/Hemingway Award nominee), *Snow, Shimoni's Lover,* and *The Sea of Light* (Lambda Literary Award finalist), and the short-story collection *Love and Death, and Other Disasters.* She has written for the *New York Times,* the *Washington Post, Rolling Stone, Mademoiselle, Forward,* and *The Advocate.* She and her partner live in Manhattan with her two sons, Makara and Vannarith, both fourteen. When Levin met them at an orphanage in Phnom Penh, Cambodia, in 1993, Mak, born with a cleft lip and palate, did not speak; Van, suffering from rickets, did not walk. Today, both boys are Little League All-Stars who refuse to let her get a word in edgewise.

ANTOINETTE MARTIN is a freelance writer and journalist based in Montclair, New Jersey. An award-winning veteran of daily newspapers in California, Connecticut, Michigan, and New Jersey, she also has written extensively for magazines. Currently, she produces a weekly real estate column for the *New York Times.* She and her ex-husband adopted Charlie, fourteen, in 1991 in Texas, and Mia, eleven, in 1993 in Michigan.

JACQUELYN MITCHARD, author of *The Deep End of the Ocean,* the first novel selected by the Oprah Winfrey Book Club, has written five other best-selling novels, including, most recently, *The Breakdown Lane.* She is the author of three children's books, the last one *Rosalie, Rosalie.* A nationally syndicated newspaper columnist, Mitchard is also a contributing editor for *Parenting* magazine. She and her husband,

Chris, live on a farm near Madison, Wisconsin. Her biological and adopted children are Rob, twenty; Dan, seventeen; Marty, fourteen; Francie, eight; Mimi, four; and Will, an infant. All four of her adoptions were done domestically.

ADAM PERTMAN's *Adoption Nation: How the Adoption Revolution Is Transforming America* was named Book of the Year by the National Adoption Foundation. He is executive director of the Evan B. Donaldson Adoption Institute, the preeminent research and policy organization in its field. Nominated for a Pulitzer Prize for his writings about adoption while a reporter and editor at the *Boston Globe*, Pertman has written commentaries for the *Los Angeles Times,* the *Baltimore Sun,* the *Miami Herald, The Christian Science Monitor,* and others. His honors include the U.S. Congress's Angel of Adoption award; the Dave Thomas Center for Adoption Law's first award for "the nation's greatest contributor to public understanding about adoption and permanency placement issues"; and the Century Foundation's Leonard Silk Journalism Award. He and his wife, Judy Baumwoll, live in Newton, Massachusetts, with their two children: Zachary, eleven, and Emilia, eight, both adopted domestically.

EMILY PRAGER is the author of *Wuhu Diary: On Taking My Adopted Daughter Back to Her Hometown in China.* Her works of fiction include the novels *Roger Fishbite* and *Eve's Tattoo,* and the short-story collection *A Visit from the Footbinder.* She has been a columnist at *The Village Voice,* the *New York Observer,* the *New York Times,* and *The Guardian* in England. In 2000, she won the first Online Journalism Award for Commentary given by the Columbia Graduate School of Journalism, for her columns on Oxygen.com. Prager and her daughter, LuLu, eleven, whom she adopted at seven months from Hefei, China, live in Manhattan.

AMY RACKEAR is a social worker whose private practice is devoted exclusively to adoption. A past president of the New York Chapter of RESOLVE, Rackear also served on the board of directors for National RESOLVE, and the New York State chapter of Families for Russian and Ukrainian Adoption (FRUA). Her essays have appeared in *News-*

week, the *New York Times,* and *Adoptive Families,* where she currently serves on the editorial advisory board. A frequent speaker at infertility and adoption conferences, she also facilitates workshops about making the transition from treatment to adoption. Rackear and her husband live in suburban New York with their fourteen-year-old son, adopted domestically, and seven-year-old daughter, adopted abroad.

BONNIE MILLER RUBIN has spent thirty years in newspapers, the last fifteen of them at the *Chicago Tribune,* where she was a member of the reporting team that won the 2001 Pulitzer Prize for explanatory journalism. She has written for numerous magazines and is a regular contributor to *Good Housekeeping.* Her many books include *Fifty on Fifty: Wisdom, Inspiration and Reflections on Women's Lives Well-Lived.* Rubin and her husband of thirty years, David, live in Flossmoor, Illinois. Their son, twenty-five, was adopted domestically; their daughter, seventeen, was adopted from Chile.

DAN SAVAGE is the author of the adoption memoir *The Kid: What Happened After My Boyfriend and I Decided to Go Get Pregnant: An Adoption Story,* which won the Pen-West Award. His other books include *Skipping Toward Gomorrah* (Lambda Literary Award) and *Savage Love,* a collection of his nationally syndicated sex advice columns. His articles about adoption have appeared in the *New York Times* and the *New York Times Magazine.* He has also written for *Travel & Leisure, Rolling Stone, Nest,* and *Salon.* The editor of *The Stranger,* Seattle's alternative newsweekly, Savage lives in Seattle with his boyfriend and their son, D.J., five, whom they adopted domestically.

BOB SHACOCHIS is the author of the novel *Swimming in the Volcano* (National Book Award finalist) and two short-story collections, *Easy in the Islands* (National Book Award) and *The Next New World* (Rome Prize in Literature). A former food columnist for *GQ,* he is a contributing editor at *Harper's, Outside,* and *Men's Journal* and has written parenting articles for *Offspring* and *Adoptive Families.* His nonfiction works include *The Immaculate Invasion* (finalist for the New Yorker Awards in Best Nonfiction of the Year) and *Domesticity: A Gastronomic*

Interpretation of Love. Bob and his wife divide their time between Florida and New Mexico. Their niece, Samantha, eighteen, who has lived with them since she was eleven, when her mother died, now attends school in California.

JILL SMOLOWE is the author of the adoption memoir *An Empty Lap: One Couple's Journey to Parenthood,* which *Reader's Digest* excerpted in both its Today's Best Nonfiction series and its magazine. An award-winning journalist, she has been on the writing staffs of the *New York Times, Newsweek,* and *Time* and is currently an associate editor at *People.* Her work has also appeared in the *Boston Globe, Adoptive Families,* and *Family Life.* She, her husband Joe Treen, and their daughter Becky, eleven, whom they adopted from China at seven months, divide their time between New Jersey and Pennsylvania's Endless Mountains.

SHEILA STAINBACK, an Emmy Award–winning TV anchor and reporter, has worked at CNBC, Fox News Channel, and Court TV. Coauthor of a chapter on women in television and news media in *Women & Men Communicating,* she has also contributed to *The Columbia Journalism Review, Essence, Adoptive Families,* and the anthology *Age Ain't Nothing But a Number.* A single mother, Stainback, and her son, Charles, six, whom she adopted as a toddler from New York's foster care system, live in Manhattan.

JOE TREEN has spent about half his career in newspapers and half in magazines. He has worked as a writer, reporter, editor, or overseas correspondent at *Newsday, Newsweek, People,* and *Discover* (where he is now editor at large) and has freelanced for the *Boston Globe,* the *Los Angeles Times, Rolling Stone, The New Republic, The Nation,* and *The Guardian.* He and his wife, writer Jill Smolowe, adopted their eleven-year-old daughter, Becky, in China when she was an infant.

JANA WOLFF is the author of *Secret Thoughts of an Adoptive Mother,* now in its fifth printing. She and her work have been featured in the *New York Times,* the *Chicago Tribune, Adoptive Families,* and on radio and television. A frequent speaker and writer on issues of adoption, race, and family, Wolff has been a keynote presenter at many national adoption conferences and serves on the board of Adopt International. She is also a ghostwriter. She and her husband, Howard, live in Honolulu, Hawaii, with their teenage son, Ari. Theirs is a transracial, open adoption.